Preface

Los! was written as a companion volume to **Fertig!** Used in parallel or sequentially they form a complete two-year course for pupils studying for the CSE or 16+ examination in German. There is considerable carry-over from one book to the other in terms of vocabulary and subject matter, but **Los!** will also usefully complement any similar CSE course.

Los! contains practice materials based on the formats of the CSE and 16+ questions most widely set by the examination boards. It also includes some materials of GCE O-level standard, where the examination format coincides with that of CSE/16+. In line with more recent practice, much of the comprehension work is based on realia and non-fictional material. In each section items are graded from the relatively simple to the more demanding. Most of the items are original, but each section contains a few examples from past papers.

However, **Los!** is more than just a collection of examination-type materials. Advice is given on how to tackle the various types of question and how to avoid the worst pitfalls. There are, in some cases, preliminary exercises, help in the form of suggested answers or approaches, suggested vocabulary, and so on. Indeed, the materials as a whole are planned to introduce pupils to a wide range of useful vocabulary and phrases, and much of the book can, I hope, be considered as a valuable teaching tool in its own right. It is hoped, therefore, that colleagues will not restrict themselves to using only those items which meet the requirements of their own particular examination board.

The tape and cassette which accompany **Los!** contain the listening comprehension material, a transcript of which is given in the teacher's section. All the short items from sections A–D are recorded twice; the longer passages and dialogues from section E are recorded once, but should be played twice.

My thanks must go to my colleagues and friends Helga Schwalm and Thomas Klare for their help with some of the comprehension material, and to Ingeborg Shackleton for checking the correctness of my German.

Contents

$\frac{lo}{85}$

Los!

practice for the CSE and 16+ examination

David Sprake
Head of Modern Languages
Wheatley Park School

Oxford University Press 1985

Oxford University Press, Walton Street, Oxford OX2 6DP

Oxford   London
New York   Toronto   Melbourne   Auckland
Kuala Lumpur   Singapore   Hong Kong   Tokyo
Delhi   Bombay   Calcutta   Madras   Karachi
Nairobi   Dar es Salaam   Cape Town

and associated companies in
Beirut   Berlin   Ibadan   Mexico City   Nicosia

Oxford is a trade mark of Oxford University Press

© Oxford University Press 1985
ISBN 0 19 912062 5

Acknowledgements

Illustrations are by Peter Bailey.

The cover photograph is by Leo Mason.

The photographs on p. 47 and 50 (top left) are by Fiona
Corbridge, on p. 50 (lower left) by Foto Studio, G. Hillis, and on
p. 50 (lower right) by Alison Souster.

The publishers would like to thank the following examinations
boards for permission to include questions from previous
examination papers:
Associated Examining Board (AEB)
Associated Lancashire Schools Examining Board (ALSEB)
East Anglian Examinations Board (EAEB)
East Midland Regional Examinations Board (EMREB)
London Regional Examining Board (LREB)
North West Regional Examinations Board (NWREB)
Northern Ireland Schools Examinations Council (NISEC)
Scottish Examination Board (SEB)
South-East Regional Examinations Board (SEREB)
Southern Regional Examinations Board (SREB)
Southern Universities' Joint Board (SUJB)
University of Cambridge Local Examinations Syndicate (UCLES)
Welsh Joint Education Committee (WJEC)
West Midlands Examinations Board (WMEB)
Yorkshire and Humberside Regional Examinations Board,
formerly West Yorkshire and Lindsay Regional Examining
Board (YHREB)

Set by Santype International Ltd., Salisbury, Wilts.
Printed in Great Britain by William Clowes Ltd., Beccles, Suffolk

Conversation

Points to remember

1 The conversation section of the examination is meant to be a conversation, and not a series of short questions and answers. The examiner will not allow you to regurgitate long, pre-learnt passages, but will give considerable credit for full, interesting answers. Think in terms of 'What does this question give me the opportunity of saying?' rather than a set answer to a particular question.

    e.g. In answer to the question „Gehen Sie oft ins Kino?", you could answer:

        „Ja."

   or „Ja, sehr oft."

   or „Ja, ich gehe sehr oft ins Kino."

   or „Ich gehe sehr gern ins Kino. Ich gehe mindestens einmal im Monat dorthin. Das nächste Kino ist nicht weit von meinem Haus. Ich gehe meistens mit meinem Freund Barry/meiner Freundin Emma dorthin. Wir sehen sehr gern Horrorfilme ..." *etc.*

2 You can make your answers full and interesting without making them complicated. Keep your answers short and simple. A good tip to remember is never to make one sentence express more than one idea. Although the examiner decides what questions to ask, you very often have a lot of freedom in how you answer. Therefore:

a Avoid difficulties such as technical terms. Simplify ideas you cannot easily express. This can be done by giving a description rather than a specific technical word:

    e.g. If your father is a wheel-tapper and shunter, say something like:

        „Mein Vater arbeitet bei der Eisenbahn. Er arbeitet am Hauptbahnhof."

b Remember that answers do not have to be factually accurate. If something is difficult, invent an alternative:

e.g. If your brother is a bank probationary securities clerk, you could simply say „Er ist Bankangestellter", or make up another job: „Er ist Verkäufer in einem großen Geschäft in der Stadt."

3 It is natural to prepare answers to questions you think are likely to be asked, but avoid the 'mini-composition' approach. Prepare in note form; this will lead to far more natural-sounding answers, you'll be much less likely to 'dry-up' in the middle of an answer, and forgetting the odd detail will not matter.

e.g. *Wrong:* „Wir wohnen in einem kleinen Reiheneckhaus in einer großen Wohnsiedlung mit ungefähr 300 Häusern in einem Vorort von Oxford ..."

Right: Ich wohne	in einem (kleinen) Haus.
Meine Familie und ich wohnen	(mitten) in einer (großen) Wohnsiedlung.
	mit (ungefähr/etwa) 200 Häusern.
Wir wohnen	nicht weit von Oxford.
	in einem Vorort von Oxford.

Conversation practice

This section helps you prepare answers to the most common questions. They are for the most part open-ended so that you can add your own individual details, and some useful vocabulary is given with each section. The **Sie** form is used for the questions; some teachers/examiners may use the **du** form.

Sie und Ihre Familie

Wie heißen Sie?
  Ich heiße ......
  Mein Name/Vorname/Nachname ist ......
Wie alt sind Sie?
  Ich bin (bald) ...... Jahre alt.
  Ich habe am ersten (zweiten, *etc.*) Januar, *etc.* Geburtstag.
Haben Sie Geschwister?

Ich habe	einen Bruder/...... Brüder.
	eine Schwester/...... Schwestern.
	keinen Bruder/keine Schwester/keine Geschwister.
	weder Brüder noch Schwestern.

Was	ist Ihr Vater/Ihre Mutter	von Beruf?
	sind Ihre Eltern	

Er/Sie ist Lehrer(in)/Arzt/Hausfrau, *etc.*
Er/Sie arbeitet zu Hause/im Büro/bei British Leyland, *etc.*
Sagen Sie mir etwas über Ihre Familie!

Mein Bruder	heißt ......
Meine Schwester	ist ...... Jahre alt.
	geht (immer noch) zur Schule/besucht diese Schule.
	ist im ersten (zweiten, *etc.*) Schuljahr.
	ist in der ersten (zweiten, *etc.*) Klasse.
	hat die Schule verlassen.
	ist verlobt/(schon/noch nicht) verheiratet.
	hat ein Kind/...... Kinder/keine Kinder.

Meine Brüder	heißen ......
Meine Schwestern	sind ......
	gehen ...... *etc.*
Wir haben	einen großen (kleinen, *etc.*) Garten.
	eine große (kleine, *etc.*) Wohnung.
	ein großes (kleines, *etc.*) Haus.

Student/–in	bei der Eisenbahn	in einem	Laden
Taxifahrer/–in	bei der Post		Geschäft
Arzt/Ärztin	in einer Fabrik	in einem Büro/Bürogebäude
Friseur/Friseuse	einem Betrieb	die Technische Hochschule
Verkäufer/–in	auf dem Bau	besuchen
Büroangestellter/–e	im Freien	auf der Uni(versität)
arbeitslos		studieren

Wo Sie wohnen

Wo wohnen Sie?

Ich wohne	in ...... (*name*)/in der Nähe
Wir wohnen	von ...... (*name*).
Meine Familie und ich wohnen	nicht weit von einem/einer/einem ......
	zwischen ...... (*name*) und ...... (*name*).
	in der Stadtmitte/in der Vorstadt.
	in einem Vorort von ...... (*name*).
	in einem Wohnblock/Hochhaus.
	in einer Wohnsiedlung/auf dem Lande/auf einem Hof.

In der Nähe von unserem Haus ist/steht/liegt/befindet sich ......

Wie ist Ihr Haus/Ihre Wohnung?
    Es/Sie ist mittelgroß/(sehr/ziemlich) klein, *etc.*
    Es/Sie hat ...... Zimmer.
    Im Erdgeschoß sind/haben wir ......
    Im ersten (zweiten, *etc.*) Stock | sind/haben wir ......
    In/Auf der ersten (zweiten, *etc.*) Etage |
    In der Küche/Im Wohnzimmer, *etc.* sind/haben wir ......
    Ich | habe mein eigenes Schlafzimmer.
         | teile mein Schlafzimmer mit ......
    Vor | dem Haus, *etc.* | ist/steht/liegt/befindet sich ......
    Hinter | | sind/stehen/liegen/befinden sich ......
Wie ist Ihr Garten?
    Wir haben | keinen Garten.
            | einen (sehr/ziemlich) kleinen, *etc.* Garten.
    Unser Garten ist (sehr/ziemlich) klein, *etc.*
    Im Vordergarten | ist/steht/liegt/befindet sich ......
    Im Hintergarten | sind/stehen/liegen/befinden sich ......
Haben Sie Haustiere?
    Nein, wir haben keine (Haustiere).
    Ja, wir haben | einen/eine/ein ......
              | zwei/ein paar/mehrere/viele ......

das Kino	die Bushaltestelle	das Gemüse
die Bäckerei	der Bahnhof	der Rasen
die Metzgerei/Fleischerei	die Omnibusstation	die Blume (–n)
der Supermarkt	der Flur	der Baum/Obstbaum (–̈e)
die Apotheke/die Drogerie	das Wohnzimmer	das Gewächshaus
die Post/das Postamt	das Eßzimmer	der Schuppen
die Bank	die Küche	die Katze (–n)
der Marktplatz	das Schlafzimmer (–)	der Hund (–e)
der Park	das Badezimmer	der Hamster (–)
das Schwimmbad	das Klo/die Toilette	das Meerschweinchen (–)
das Sportzentrum	das Obst	das Kaninchen (–)

Das Datum/der Tag/die Uhrzeit/das Wetter

Der wievielte ist heute? Den wievielten haben wir heute?/Welches
Datum ist/haben wir heute?
    Heute | ist der erste (zweite, *etc.*) Mai, *etc.*
         | haben wir den ersten (zweiten, *etc.*) Mai, *etc.*

Welcher Tag ist heute?

    Heute ist Montag, *etc.*

Wie spät ist es?/Wieviel Uhr ist es?

    Es ist | (fast/ungefähr) zehn Uhr, *etc.* (morgens/vormittags).
           | (schon) halb drei, *etc.* (nachmittags).

Wann?/Um wieviel Uhr (stehen Sie auf, *etc.*)?

    Um sieben Uhr (stehe ich auf, *etc.*)

Wie ist das Wetter heute?

    Heute | regnet es (stark/in Strömen)/schneit es/gewittert es/friert es.
          | ist es (ein bißchen/sehr) windig/nebelig.
          | ist das Wetter (nicht besonders) warm/(ziemlich) kalt/(zu) heiß.
          | scheint die Sonne.

Wie war das Wetter gestern?

    Gestern | hat es geregnet/geschneit/gewittert/gefroren.
            | war es windig, *etc.*
            | war das Wetter kalt, *etc.*

(im) Januar		September	Freitag	regnerisch			
Februar		Oktober	Samstag	eiskalt			
März		November	Sonnabend	dicht			
April		Dezember	Sonntag	tief			
Mai	(am) Montag		der Wind	mit	Eis		bedeckt
Juni		Dienstag	der Regen		Schnee		
Juli		Mittwoch	der Schnee				
August		Donnerstag	der Nebel				

Die Schule

Wie kommen Sie zur Schule?

    Normalerweise laufe ich zur Schule.

    Ich komme/gehe zu Fuß zur Schule.

    Ich komme/fahre auf meinem Rad/mit dem Schulbus.

    Mein Vater/Meine Mutter bringt mich mit dem Auto zur Schule.

Was für eine Schule besuchen Sie?

    Es ist eine Gesamtschule/ein Gymnasium/ein Internat, *etc.*

    Sie | ist | (ziemlich/sehr) klein/groß.
    Es | | mittelgroß/riesengroß/enorm (groß).
        | hat | ...... Lehrerinnen und Lehrer/Lehrkräfte.
            | ...... Klassenzimmer.

    Es gibt ...... Unterichtsstunden/Pausen, *etc.* am/pro Tag.

    Eine Unterrichtsstunde/Eine Pause, *etc.* dauert ...... Minuten.

    Die erste Stunde/Die Mittagspause dauert von ...... bis ......

Wie ist Ihre Schuluniform?

> Wir | haben keine (Schuluniform).
> | müssen/sollen einen blauen Pullover, *etc.* tragen.
> | dürfen keine Jeans, *etc.* tragen.

Gehen Sie gern zur Schule?

> Ja(wohl)!/Sicher!/Aber natürlich!/Selbstverständlich!
> Nein!/Nicht besonders (gern)/Gar nicht gern!/Um Gottes willen nicht!/ Bestimmt nicht!/Ganz im Gegenteil!

Was lernen Sie in der Schule?

> Ich lerne Mathe, *etc.*
> Ich mag gern/lieber/am liebsten Englisch, *etc.*
> Mein Lieblingsfach ist Französisch/Deutsch, *etc.*
> Ich interessiere mich (sehr/gar nicht) für Sport/Turnen, *etc.*
> Ich bin (sehr/ziemlich) gut | in Erdkunde/
> (ein bißchen/etwas) schwach | Geschichte, *etc.*

Wie heißen/sind Ihre Lehrerinnen und Lehrer?

> Mein(e) Deutschlehrer(in) | heißt ......
> Der Schulleiter/Die Schulleiterin | ist ......
> Mein(e) Klassenlehrer(in) |
> Er/Sie ist | nett/sympathisch/freundlich/streng/langweilig.
> | ein guter *etc.* Lehrer/eine gute *etc.* Lehrerin.

die Hose (–n)	die Fremdsprache (–n)	Kunst
die Socke (–n)	Religion	Hauswirtschaft
der Schuh (–e)	Werkunterricht	das Motorrad (–̈er)
die Jacke (–n)	Englische Literatur	das Moped/Mofa (–s)
der Rock (–̈e)	Physik	die U-Bahn
die Krawatte (–n)	Chemie	der Zug
das Kleid (–er)	Biologie	
die Bluse (–n)	Musik	

Die tägliche Routine

Was machen Sie, bevor Sie in die Schule kommen?

> Ich | stehe auf.
> | wasche mich.
> | ziehe mich an.
> | frühstücke (in der Küche, *etc.*/mit meinen Eltern, *etc.*).
> Dann | suche ich meine Schulsachen zusammen.
> | verlasse ich das Haus.
> | mache ich mich auf den Weg (zur Schule).

10

Was haben Sie heute früh gemacht?

Ich | bin um sieben Uhr, *etc.* aufgestanden.
| habe mich gewaschen/habe mich angezogen.
| habe gefrühstückt/habe ...... gegessen/habe ...... getrunken.

Dann | bin ich zur Haltestelle gegangen.
| habe ich auf den Bus gewartet.

Was werden Sie wohl heute abend machen?

Ich werde | mich umziehen.
| meine Hausaufgaben machen.
| (mir) ein paar Platten anhören.
| zu Hause bleiben und fernsehen.

Wahrscheinlich | werde ich | ausgehen (können).
Vielleicht | | in eine Disko gehen.
Hoffentlich | | mich mit der Clique treffen.

aufwachen	eine Zeitschrift lesen		sich ausziehen
(sich) duschen	einen Brief schreiben		Radio hören
ein Bad nehmen	mit	einem Freund	ausgehen	ins/zu Bett gehen
sich ausruhen		einer Freundin		sich hinlegen

Hobbys und Freizeitsbeschäftigungen

Was machen Sie in Ihrer Freizeit?

Ich | gehe (sehr selten/oft/am Abend, *etc.*) aus.
| bleibe (meistens/manchmal/nicht oft/nie, *etc.*) zu Hause.
| sehe (wenig/viel) fern.

Am Wochenende gehe ich zu Partys/Diskos.

Wofür/Für was interessieren Sie sich?

Ich interessiere mich für Sport/Musik, *etc.*
Ich schwärme für Tanzen, *etc.*

Sind Sie Sportler(in)?

Nein, ich treibe nicht viel/keinen Sport.
Ja, ich spiele gern Fußball, *etc.*

Welche Hobbys haben Sie?

Ich habe keine (Hobbys).
Ich sammle Briefmarken/Posters, *etc.*
Ich lese/schwimme gern.

Wie oft gehen Sie ins Kino/in den Jugendklub?

Ich gehe einmal/zweimal in der Woche/im Monat dorthin.

Mit wem?

    Mit meinem Freund/meiner Freundin/meinen Freunden, *etc.*

Was für Filme sehen Sie gern?

    Ich mag gern/lieber/am liebsten Horrorfilme, *etc.*

    Liebesfilme, *etc.* mag ich nicht.

    Ich kann Schnulzen, *etc.* nicht leiden.

Sind Sie musikalisch?

    Nein, ich spiele kein Instrument.

    Ja, ich spiele Klavier/Gitarre, *etc.*

    Ich mag/höre gern Popmusik/klassische Musik.

Bekommen Sie Taschengeld?

    Nein, ich bekomme/kriege keins!

    Ja, ich bekomme/kriege ...... Pfund pro Woche.

    Ich | verdiene auch noch Geld dazu.

         | trage Zeitungen aus.

         | arbeite | als Babysitter/Tankwart, *etc.*

                   | in einem Supermarkt, *etc.*

Was kaufen Sie damit?

    Ich | spare ...... Pfund davon.

         | kaufe mir Kleidung/Klamotten/Cassetten/Platten, *etc.*

Was (für Kleidung) tragen Sie am Wochenende?

    Ich trage (normalerweise/meistens) Jeans, eine Lederjacke, *etc.*

das Eislaufen	das Fotographieren	ins Theater gehen	der Schlager (–)
das Eisstadion	angeln	das Popkonzert (–e)	die Hitparade (–n)
das Hallenbad	basteln	der Bierdeckel (–)	die Geige (–n)
das Radfahren	der Lustspielfilm (–e)	die Münze (–n)	die Trompete (–n)
das Pferdereiten	der Spionagefilm (–e)	das Mitglied (–er)	üben
reiten	das Musical (–s)	die Mannschaft (–en)	der Pulli (–s)
spazierengehen	das Magazin (–e)	der Sportverein (–e)	das T-shirt (–s)
spazierenfahren	der Roman (–e)	trainieren	

Ferienzeit

Wo verbringen Sie normalerweise Ihre Ferien?

    Wir verbringen sie meistens | in Schottland/London/Cornwall, *etc.*

                             | in Nordengland/Südfrankreich, *etc.*

                             | in der Schweiz.

    Normalerweise fahren wir | nach Schottland/London/Cornwall, *etc.*

                             | nach Nordengland/Südfrankreich, *etc.*

                             | in die Schweiz.

Gewöhnlich fliegen wir nach Spanien, *etc.*

Zu	Weihnachten	bleiben wir zu Hause.	
	Ostern	fahren wir zu Freunden/Verwandten.	
	Pfingsten		
Die	Weihnachtsferien	verbringen wir	zu Hause.
	Osterferien		bei Freunden/Verwandten.
	Pfingstferien		

Und voriges/letztes Jahr?

Wir	waren voriges/letztes Jahr in Schottland, *etc.*	
	sind voriges/letztes Jahr nach Spanien, *etc.*	gefahren.
		geflogen.

Wir haben	eine Woche	in Deutschland, *etc.* verbracht.
	vierzehn Tage, *etc.*	

Ich bin	nach Cornwall	getrampt.
	durch ganz Europa	

Erzählen Sie mir etwas über Ihren Aufenthalt/Ihre Ferien!

Wir	sind am ersten August, *etc.* abgefahren.
	haben uns drei Tage, *etc.* in ...... aufgehalten.
	sind eine Woche, *etc.* in ...... geblieben.
	haben	Denkmäler/Ruinen/einen Dom, *etc.* besichtigt.
		eine Burg/ein Museum, *etc.* besucht.
		in der See gebadet.
		einen Ausflug nach ...... gemacht.
		eine Dampferfahrt/Hafenrundfahrt gemacht.
Wir haben	in einem Hotel/einer Pension übernachtet.
	im Wohnwagen gewohnt.
	gezeltet.

Waren Sie schon einmal in Deutschland/in Österreich/in der Schweiz?

Nein, ich	war noch nie dort.
	bin noch nie dorthin gefahren.
Ja, ich war	schon einmal/zweimal, *etc.* dort.
	voriges Jahr/vor zwei Jahren, *etc.* dort.

Ich habe an einem Schüleraustausch mit einer deutschen Schule teilgenommen.

Was haben Sie für die kommenden Sommerferien vor?

Ich habe noch keine Ferienpläne.

Ich	werde wahrscheinlich/hoffentlich ins Ausland, *etc.* fahren.	
	hoffe	an die Costa Brava, *etc.*	zu fliegen.
		nach Spanien *etc.*	fliegen zu können.
		vierzehn Tage in Mallorca, *etc.* zu verbringen.	

mit	dem Schiff	unterwegs		Nord____
	der Fähre	auf dem Weg nach		Süd____
	dem Flugzeug	über Köln *etc.* fahren		Ost____
	dem Hovercraft	ins Ausland	fahren	West____
den Kanal überqueren		aufs Land		Nordwest____*etc.*
die Überfahrt		ins Grüne		Italien
still/stürmisch		an die See/Küste		Irland
seekrank		ans Meer		Wales

Die Zukunft

Was werden Sie wohl machen, wenn Sie | die Schule verlassen?
| mit der Schule fertig sind?

Ich | weiß es noch nicht.
| habe (bisher) keine festen Pläne.

Ich | werde wohl in einem Geschäft, *etc.* | arbeiten.
| möchte gern | in der Großstadt
| | im Ausland

Ich | möchte (einmal) Lehrer(in), *etc.* werden.
| hoffe (einmal) Büroangestellte(r) zu werden.

Ich hoffe | zu studieren.
| studieren zu dürfen.

die Oberstufe	in einer Fabrik	arbeiten
die Fachoberschule	in einem Betrieb	
die Technische Hochschule	in einem Büro	
auf der/die Uni(versität)	auf dem Feld	
einen festen Job bekommen	auf dem Bau	
eine (gutbezahlte) Stellung finden	stempelngehen	
einen Beruf wählen	auswandern	
der Lehrling (–e)		

14

Role-play

Points to remember

1 If you are supposed to be speaking to a 'correspondent', a 'friend', or a 'youngster', remember to address him/her as **du**:

    „**Kannst du** mir helfen?"

    „**Komm** mit! ... Ich zeige **dir**, wo es ist."

When speaking or referring to more than one of the above remember to use the **ihr** form:

    „**Könnt** ihr mir helfen?"

    „**Kommt** mit! ... Ich zeige **euch**, wo es ist."

  When you are supposed to be speaking to 'strangers' or grown-ups such as 'correspondent's parents' or 'teachers', remember to use **Sie**:

    „**Können Sie** mir helfen?"

    „**Kommen Sie** mit! ... Ich zeige **Ihnen**, wo es ist."

2 Always be formal when addressing and taking leave of 'strangers':

    „Entschuldigen Sie, bitte ..."

    „Guten | Tag. | Können Sie mir bitte helfen?"
              | Abend. |

    „Vielen Dank (für Ihre Hilfe)."

3 A bad mistake to make is to try to translate the actual wording of the instructions given on your role-play card. Provided you manage to communicate the information, you are free to choose the way you phrase the sentences/questions. There are usually several, equally acceptable, ways of doing this. Only use what you know you can handle! Here are three examples of typical instructions and the different ways of dealing with them:

15

> *You are in a German town. You speak to a passer-by:*
> *Ask him/her the way to the Tourist Information Office.*

You could say:

„Entschuldigen Sie, bitte. Können Sie mir bitte helfen? Ich bin fremd hier. Wissen Sie vielleicht, wo sich die Tourist-Informationsstelle befindet?"

But you could also say:

„Wie komme ich am besten zur Tourist-Informationsstelle?"

„Wo ist die Tourist-Informationsstelle, bitte?"

„Gibt es in der Nähe eine Tourist-Informationstelle?"

„Ich suche die Tourist-Informationsstelle."

> *You are on a train. You speak to a fellow-passenger:*
> *Ask him/her if he/she knows how much longer it's going to take to get to Nürnberg.*

You could say:

„Entschuldigen Sie, bitte. Wissen Sie, wie lange es noch dauert, bis wir in Nürnberg ankommen?"

But you could also say:

„Ist es noch weit bis Nürnberg?"

„Ich steige in Nürnberg aus. Ist das noch weit?"

„Wissen Sie, um wieviel Uhr wir in Nürnberg ankommen?"

„Wann sind wir in Nürnberg?"

> *You are at a party with your correspondent.*
> *Tell him/her you feel ill and want to go home.*

You could say:

„Ich fühle mich ein bißchen unwohl. Es tut mir leid aber ich möchte lieber nach Hause gehen. Ich hoffe, das macht dir nichts aus."

But you could also say:

„Ich fühle mich nicht wohl. Bitte laß uns nach Hause gehen!"

„Mir ist gar nicht gut. Ich möchte bitte heimgehen."

„Mir ist schlecht. Könnten wir vielleicht nach Hause gehen?"

„Es geht mir nicht gut und ich muß nach Hause."

„Ich bin krank. Ich will nach Hause (gehen)."

Useful structures

The following structures will help you to deal with most of the instructions/situations you are likely to encounter:

Das ist/sind ...... This is/These are ......
Ist/Sind das ......? Is this/Are these ......?
Wie geht es + *dative*? How is ......?
Ich habe ...... I've got ......
Haben Sie ......?, *etc.* Have you got ......?
Es gibt ...... There is ....../There are ......
Gibt es (in der Nähe) ......? Is there a ....../Are there any ...... (near here)?
Wo ist (der/die/das nächste) ......? Where is (the nearest/next) ......?
Ich will ...... + *inf.* I want to ......
Wollen Sie ...... + *inf.*? Do you want to ......?
Ich möchte ...... + *inf.* I'd like to ......
Möchten Sie ...... + *inf.*? Would you like to ......?
Darf ich ...... + *inf.*? May I ......?/Am I allowed to ......?
Sie dürfen (nicht) ...... + *inf.* You are(n't) allowed to ......
Kann ich ...... + *inf.*? Can I ......?
Sie können ...... + *inf.* You can ......
Könnte ich ...... + *inf.*? Could I ......?
Könnten Sie ...... + *inf.*? Could you ......?
Soll ich ...... + *inf.*? Am I supposed to ......?
Sie sollen ...... + *inf.* You are supposed to ......
Sollte ich ...... + *inf.*? Should I ......?
Sie sollten ...... + *inf.* You should ......
Muß ich ...... + *inf.*? Must I ......?
Sie müssen ...... + *inf.* You must ...... '
Ich würde (lieber) ...... + *inf.* I'd (rather) ......
Würden Sie (bitte) ...... + *inf.*? Would you (kindly) ......?
Ich hoffe, ... zu + *inf.* I'm hoping to ......
Ich habe vor, ... zu + *inf.* I intend to ......
Ich werde (wohl/wahrscheinlich) ...... + *inf.* I shall (probably) ......
Ich | **brauche ......** | I | need ......
    | **suche ......** | am looking for ......
Was kostet/kosten ......? How much is/are ......?
Ich nehme bitte ...... I'll take ......
Ich möchte auch noch ...... I'd also like ......
Geben Sie | **mir bitte ......** Please | give | me ......
Bringen Sie | | bring |

Können Sie mir ...... empfehlen? Can you recommend me ......?
Laß/Laßt/Lassen Sie uns ......! Let's ......!
Wann fährt der/die/das nächste ...... nach ...... ab? When does the next ...... leave for ......?
Ich (*verb*)–e (nicht) gern ...... I (don't) like ____ing.
Ich (*verb*)–e lieber ...... I('d) prefer to ......
Am liebsten (*verb*)–e ich ...... Most of all I('d) like to ......
...... gefällt/gefallen mir. I like ......
...... schmeckt mir (nicht). I (don't) like the taste of ......
Ich mag | **...... (nicht).** I (don't) like ......
       | **kein(e)(n) ......**
Ich interessiere mich für ...... I'm interested in ......
...... interessiert/interessieren mich (nicht). ...... interest(s)/do(es)n't interest me.
Ich habe (keine) Lust, ... zu + *inf*. I (don't) fancy ____ing.
Haben/Hätten Sie Lust, ... zu + *inf*.? Do/Would you fancy ____ing?
Wo ist/sind ......? Where is/are ......?
Wie komme ich am besten | **zum/zur/zum ......?** How do I get to ......?
       | **nach ......?**
Ich zeige Ihnen, *etc.* | **wo ......** I'll show you | where ......
       | **wie ......** *etc.* | | how ......
Es tut mir leid (, ich kann nicht ...... *etc.***)** I'm sorry (I can't ......)
Leider (kann ich nicht ......, *etc.***)** Unfortunately (I can't ......)
Paßt/Passen mir ......? Do(es) ...... suit me?
Steht/Stehen mir ......? Do(es) ...... fit me?
Was für ......? What sort/kind of ......?
Ich habe ...... | **verloren.** | I've | lost ......
       | **verlegt.** | | mislaid ......
       | **vergessen.** | | forgotten ......
       | **liegen lassen.** | | left ......
Ich kann ...... nicht finden. I can't find ......

Ich weiß nicht	**, ob ......(?)**	I don't know	whether ......(?)
Wissen Sie, *etc.*	**, wann ......(?)**	Do you know	when ......(?)
Ich habe keine Ahnung	**, wo ......,** *etc.* **(?)**	I haven't a clue	where, *etc.* ......(?)
Können Sie, *etc.*, **mir sagen**		Can you tell me	

Ich verstehe nicht (, wie ...... *etc.***)** I don't understand (how ......, *etc.*).
Etwas ist mit + *dative* nicht in Ordnung. Something's wrong with the ...
Mir | **tut der/die/das ...... weh.** | My ...... hurt(s).
      | **tun die ......**

Role-play situations

This section reviews the most common topic areas and offers a wide variety of practice items of the kind you will be required to deal with. Each section begins with a typical examination role-play card including the sort of replies/reactions you can expect from the teacher/examiner. This is followed by other information you may be required to give, or seek, under the topic in question.

1 Initial contact

> *You have just met your correspondent Karl/Helga at the station. Your teacher will play the part of the correspondent:*
>
> − Greet your correspondent and introduce your parents, brother and sister.
> − Freut mich sehr!
> − Offer to take his/her case and bag.
> − Gerne!
> − Ask what the journey was like.
> − Es war ein bißchen anstrengend.

Introduce yourself, give your age and say you are English, Scottish, *etc.* Say where you come from.
Ask someone's name, how old he/she is and whether he/she is German, Swiss, or Austrian. Ask where he/she comes from.
Say where you are staying and for how long. Say which members of your family are with you.
Ask where someone is staying in England, *etc.*, and for how long. Ask whether he/she is on his/her own or with family, friends, *etc.*
Welcome some German guests who arrive at your home. Ask them in and invite them to sit down. Tell them where the bathroom/toilet is. Ask whether they are tired. Ask whether they are hungry/thirsty. Say you'll get them something to drink. Ask what they'd like: tea? coffee? Ask whether they'd like to eat straight away or later in the evening. Ask whether they'd like to have a shower/bath and get changed. Say you'll show them where their rooms are.
You arrive in a German person's home: Say you're pleased to be there/to meet them/to see them again. Say what sort of a journey you had.
Apologize for arriving later than expected and explain why.

19

(train/plane/boat was late? breakdown? heavy traffic?) Say you're tired/(not) a bit hungry/you'd like something to drink. Say you'd like a shower/wash/bath/to get changed. Ask where the bathroom/toilet/your room is. Say you'd like to unpack; you have some presents in your case. Distribute the presents to the members of the family. Say you'd like an early night after your long journey.

2 In the family

You are staying with a German family. You are speaking to your correspondent's mother. Your teacher will play the part of the mother:

- Ask whether the postman has been yet.
- Ja, schon vor einer Viertelstunde.
- Ask whether there was anything for you.
- Nein, leider nicht.
- Ask whether you can have some writing paper and an envelope as you'd like to write to your parents.
- Aber selbstverständlich!

Say you slept very well; the bed was very comfortable and it's a lovely room.

Ask whether your correspondent slept well. Tell him/her there is a card/letter for him/her from Germany/Switzerland, *etc*. Tell him/her what there is for breakfast. Ask whether he/she would like a cooked breakfast. Ask him/her if he/she has everything he/she needs (more milk? sugar? butter? *etc*.).

Say you have forgotten to bring a towel/flannel and ask whether you can borrow one. Ask if you may use the toothpaste/hairdrier. Ask if they have a spare toothbrush/comb/hairbrush. Ask for some more soap/toilet paper. Ask your correspondent what he's/she's looking for. Ask if he/she needs something and whether you can lend him/her whatever it is. Ask whether he/she has any dirty washing; say it's no problem as it can go into the machine with the family wash. Say that his/her shirt/blouse *etc*. is washed and ironed.

Say you have some dirty washing. Say you'll do it yourself if you can have some washing powder.

Answer the phone; explain that you are the son's/daughter's English *etc*. correspondent; explain that the family is out at the moment and say when they are due back.

Offer to help with the washing-up, *etc.* Ask your correspondent if he/she will help you tidy up your room.

Ask whether he/she has written to his/her parents yet. Say that he/she can get postcards in a nearby shop. Say you can let him/her have some stamps.

Ask whether you can buy cards/stamps nearby.

Ask whether you can watch television. Ask whether they know what is on this evening. Ask where the newspaper is. Ask whether you can play some records/borrow a book/magazine.

3 Making arrangements

> *You are arranging to meet a German friend in town. Your teacher will play the part of your German friend:*
>
> – Ask where you are supposed to meet him/her.
> – Kommt d'rauf an, wie gut du die Stadt kennst.
> – Say you know where the town hall is.
> – Das wär' ein guter Treffpunkt.
> – Ask at what time you should be there.
> – Sagen wir um sechs Uhr!

Ask where the phone book/code book is. Ask whether someone knows the STD code for Cologne, etc. Ask whether they know someone's phone number (e.g. Karl's, Inge Schmidt's).

Dial Directory Enquiries: say you want a number in Switzerland. Say the person is living with the Steger family in Bockenbühl (Spell this name!) near Basel; give the address (St. Bonifaziusstraße 83). Ask whether you can dial this number direct from Germany.

Phone a German friend's home, give your name, and ask whether Rainer/Monika is there. Say you want him/her to meet you in town tomorrow morning; ask the person to tell him/her to phone you back. Give your number (6 98 64).

Ask your correspondent where he/she would like to go this evening/tomorrow/at the weekend. Ask whether he/she would like to go with you to a disco/a party/into town/for a walk.

Explain to your correspondent that you have to go and see one of your teachers; tell him/her you'll meet him/her here/in front of the school/in your classroom in ten minutes/a quarter of an hour/half an hour.

Phone and say you'd like an appointment with the doctor/dentist as soon as possible. Accept a certain day/date and time. (Repeat it to confirm.) Say you're sorry but the day/date/time offered is no good; explain why (another appointment? going on an outing? *etc.*); ask whether they can offer you an alternative.

Phone and book a table for a certain number of people for a certain time and evening. Give your surname. (Spell it to be sure they get it right!)

Say you're going out, where you're going and what time you expect to be back. Ask your correspondent what time he is going to be back this evening.

4 In the street

> *You are driving in Germany and stop to speak to a passer-by. Your teacher will play the part of the passer-by:*
>
> – Say excuse me and ask whether this is the right way into the town centre.
> – Ja! Fahren Sie immer geradeaus!
> – Ask whether it is easy to park there.
> – Ja, sicher. Es gibt zwei große Parkhäuser dort.
> – Ask whether you can get petrol somewhere nearby.
> – Gleich um die Ecke.

Ask the name of the town you are in. Ask someone to show you on the map where Schönfeld is/to show you on your town plan where a certain place is (e.g. the town hall). Ask how much further it is to a certain town. Ask how to get to the nearest car park/underground station/bank/post office/ petrol station/garage. Ask where the tourist office/market-place/ toilets/bus station is/are.

Ask where you can get a newspaper around here. Ask whether there is a good, cheap restaurant nearby. Ask someone whether he/she knows where the Hotel Adler is. Ask whether the Beethovenstraße is the first, second or third street and whether it's on the left or right. Ask what a certain building is.

Tell someone to turn left/right/take the first/second/third turning to the left/right; tell them to go straight on/go over the bridge/turn left at the traffic lights/turn right at the crossroads. Ask whether you are allowed to park here.

22

5 Shopping

You are in a clothes shop. Your teacher will play the part of the shop assistant:

- Tell the assistant you'd like to try on a certain pair of trousers/jeans.
- Die Umkleidekabinen sind um die Ecke.
- Say you like them very much but they don't fit you; they are too tight.
- Ach, wie schade!
- Ask whether they have the same ones in a larger size.
- Leider nicht.

You are serving a German customer: Ask if you can help him/her. Ask what he/she is looking for. Ask how much he/she is thinking of paying.
Ask a shop assistant whether he/she has a certain article/commodity (e.g. envelopes, flip-flops, English newspapers, a film for your camera, a battery for your watch). Ask how much something costs (e.g. the sunglasses, coffee, watch straps).
Ask for a certain quantity of a certain commodity (e.g. a kilo of apples, bottle of Coke, small tube of toothpaste, four peaches).
Ask whether they have any other postcards/posters, *etc.* Ask whether they have a certain article in a different size, colour or material (e.g. this T-shirt in blue, these boots in a smaller size, this jacket in leather).
Say something is a bit expensive; ask whether they have a cheaper one.
Ask the assistant whether he/she can recommend presents for various people (e.g. 12 year-old brother, mother).
Say you'll take a certain article and ask for it to be gift-wrapped.
Say you're returning an article; say when you bought it and explain what's wrong with it (zip broken? doesn't work?). Ask if you can have a refund.
Ask if they can recommend another shop where you might be able to get a certain article (i.e. which they haven't got in stock).
Apologize and say you haven't anything smaller than a DM100 note.
Say that they have given you the wrong change.

6 School

> *You are in your correspondent's school in Germany. You are*
> *speaking to a German teacher. Your teacher will play the part of*
> *the teacher:*
>
> – Ask the teacher where the toilets are.
> – Am Ende des Gangs ... Bist du neu in der Schule?
> – Explain that you are English and that you're Peter/Birgit
>   Schmidt's correspondent.
> – Was hältst du denn von unserer Schule?
> – Say you think it's fantastic; so modern and well-equipped. Say
>   you're very impressed!

Tell your correspondent he/she can borrow your brother's/sister's bike to
ride to school on. Tell him/her what time you have to catch the school bus.
Ask him/her how he/she gets to school in Germany.
Give him/her full details about the coming school day (i.e. when school
begins and ends, what lessons you have, how long they last, when and
how long the breaks are). Ask questions about the coming school day (i.e.
when school begins and ends, *etc.*). Ask him/her about his/her favourite
lessons. Tell him/her what you think about the various subjects you take.
Ask him/her what his/her teachers are like. Ask whether his/her English
teacher is male or female. Tell him/her what your various teachers are like.
Ask where the library/cloakrooms/school office is/are.
Ask whether he/she has a lot of homework tonight.

7 In the post office, bank, exchange office

> *You are in a post office in Germany. Your teacher will play the*
> *part of the counter clerk:*
>
> – Say you'd like to send a parcel to Great Britain.
> – Ich wiege es mal ... DM4,80.
> – Ask how long it will take to get there.
> – Na ja. Das ist nicht sicher. Fünf bis sieben Tage, nehme ich an.
> – Ask if he/she will give you some two Mark pieces in your change.
> – Aber natürlich!

Ask how much it costs to send a card/letter to Great Britain. Ask for one
DM1,20 stamp and five DM0,80 stamps.

24

Ask for a postal order for DM80.

Ask what the exchange rate is. Say you'd like to cash £30 worth of traveller's cheques/change £40 into Marks. Say how you'd like DM200 to be paid out (e.g. two DM50 notes, two DM20 notes, four DM10 notes and the rest in change). Say you've forgotten your passport/left your passport at the hotel. Say you have your driver's licence/medical card/no identification with you. Ask where you have to sign.

Say you don't understand a certain form/a certain word on a form (e.g. Wohnort, Postleitzahl)/the telephone instructions. Ask if he/she will explain it to you/help you.

8 Petrol station, garage

You are on holiday with your family in Germany when your car breaks down. You phone a garage. Your teacher will play the part of the garage proprietor:

- Explain that you are a British tourist and that you have broken down. Ask whether they can send a mechanic.
- Wo sind Sie eigentlich?
- Say you are between Poggendorf and Litzenheim on the Bundesstraße 263 and give further details (e.g. opposite a church/in a lay-by).
- Um was für ein Auto handelt es sich?
- Tell him/her what kind of car it is.

Ask for a certain amount of low/high grade petrol (e.g. full tank/30 litres/DM100's worth).

Ask the attendant to check the water/tyres/oil. Say the tyre pressure should be 1,8 front and 2,4 rear.

Ask whether there are any toilets. Ask whether they sell soft drinks.

Ask if they have a workshop. Say there is something wrong with your brakes/steering/clutch/the exhaust pipe is loose/the engine is overheating. Ask if they can do the work straight away. If not, ask when it can be done/if they can recommend another garage. Ask for a rough estimate of the cost. Say you are insured with the AA (an organization like the German ADAC) and that you have some documents in German which explain the situation.

Ask whether they can repair a puncture for you/sell you a new tyre.

Ask whether they can hire you a car. Say how long you'll need it for. Ask how much it will be.

9 Illness

You are staying with a German family. Your teacher will play the part of your correspondent's mother:

- Tell your correspondent's mother that you don't feel very well; you feel sick and have a headache.
- Sollte ich vielleicht den Arzt kommen lassen?
- Say you don't think that's necessary, but ask if it's all right for you to stay in bed today.
- Aber natürlich. Möchtest du etwas essen oder trinken?
- Say you don't want anything to eat or drink, but that you'd like some aspirin or something similar.
- Ich bringe dir gleich etwas.

Ring the doctor's surgery and explain your situation (e.g. British tourist/pupil on exchange trip) and say you'll be in Germany for another ten days. Ask whether you can see the doctor.

Tell the doctor what your symptoms are (e.g. temperature, sickness, dizziness, loss of appetite, pains in stomach, sore throat, earache, headache, insomnia). Tell him/her what you have been eating and drinking over the past couple of days.

Tell him/her where you have a pain. Say your ankle/knee/wrist is swollen; say you hurt it playing tennis.

Tell the dentist's assistant you have a bad toothache/have lost a filling/have chipped a tooth. Ask how soon you can see the dentist.

Ask the chemist if he/she can give you something for sunburn/diarrhoea/ constipation/a rash/a wasp sting/an insect bite/a bad cough/a bad cold/the flu. Ask for a bandage/sticking plaster/safety pins.

10 Eating out

You go to a German restaurant with your family. Your teacher will play the part of the waiter/waitress:

- Ask if they have a table for four.
- Wenn Sie mir folgen wollen, meine Herrschaften.
- Say you'd prefer to have a table near the window.
- Aber selbstverständlich.
- Ask for the menu and the wine list.
- Ich bringe Sie Ihnen gleich.

Say you reserved a table earlier in the day by phone in the name of X.
Order a three-course meal for yourself and a friend.
Order drinks (e.g. a bottle of red wine and a beer).
Order three coffees, a piece of fruit flan with whipped cream, a piece of
Black Forest gateau and an ice cream.
Ask if you could have some more bread (rolls)/water/butter/another bottle
of wine. Ask for some salt/pepper/mustard/vinegar/ketchup.
Ask if you could have another knife/fork/spoon/plate/glass, as this one is
dirty.
Ask for the bill/Say you'd like to pay now. Tell the waiter/waitress to keep
the change. Say you think there is a mistake in the bill. Ask him/her for
your coats. Say you enjoyed the meal; it was a very pleasant evening.

11 Travel

> *You are going through German/Swiss/Austrian customs. Your
> teacher will play the part of the customs official:*
>
> – Haben Sie etwas zu verzollen?
> – Say that in the suitcase you have a bottle of wine and a bottle of
>   whisky as presents for the German family you are going to visit.
> – Und Zigaretten?
> – Say you haven't any cigarettes; you don't smoke, neither do your
>   German friends.
> – Und in der Tasche?
> – Say you have a couple of LPs, a book about London, and some
>   English sweets and chocolate; apart from that just personal
>   clothes and belongings.
> – Bitte schön ... Sie können gehen.

Say you'd like a certain number of first/second class single/return tickets
to a certain destination.
Ask when the next bus/tram/train/boat leaves for a certain destination/
arrives from a certain place. Ask when your train/boat/plane
arrives/docks/lands. Ask what sort of train it is (stopping train? express?).
Ask what platform it leaves from/arrives at. Ask whether the train from
Munich/BA flight 209 from Gatwick is on time/will be late. Ask how late it is
expected to be.
Ask whether there is anywhere you can leave your luggage for a couple of
hours. Ask where the waiting-room is. Ask if there is somewhere you can

change some money.

Ask if this bus/tram goes to the main station/market-place/into the town centre. Ask how many tickets you require. Ask whether they are single or return tickets.

Ask if the next train to Bonn is direct or whether you have to change, and if so, where.

Ask from which deck passengers will be disembarking.

Ask if a certain seat is free. Tell someone the seat he/she has taken is reserved and show him/her your reservation. Tell an official that all of the seats seem to be reserved and ask where there are any unreserved ones.

Ask if there is a restaurant car on the train. Ask how to get to the bar/cafeteria/purser's office. Say you'd like to reserve a certain number of seats/couchettes/cabins.

Make enquiries about travelling from Bonn to Berlin by coach (e.g. if it's cheaper than by train, how much the fare is, departure/arrival times, how long the journey takes). Ask what documents you'll require. Ask if you'll need to reserve a seat.

Explain that you have lost your ticket.

12 Accommodation

> *You are looking for accommodation in Germany. You go into an hotel. Your teacher will play the part of the receptionist:*
>
> − Ask whether he/she has a room free.
> − Leider sind wir momentan völlig ausgebucht.
> − Ask if he/she could recommend another hotel in the vicinity.
> − Sie könnten das Gasthaus „Zur Weißen Taube" versuchen. Das ist aber ziemlich weit weg von hier.
> − Ask if you can use his/her phone to give them a ring.
> − Bitte schön.

Say good evening and book a certain number of single and/or double rooms; say how many nights you wish to stay. Specify rooms with shower or bathroom/toilet. Ask what the rates are (per person? per room?).

Ask if they serve meals/drinks in the hotel. If not, ask if there's a good, cheap snack-bar/restaurant in the vicinity. Ask what time breakfast/the evening meal is served. Ask if it's too late to eat there this evening/if you could have a meal in your room.

Say you like the town/region and ask if it's possible to stay an extra night. Ask whether they have any tent/caravan sites free. Ask what their rates are.

Say how many cars/tents/caravans you have and how many adults and children you are.
Ask if you can change rooms/sites and explain why (traffic noise? uneven ground? smell from dustbins?).
Ask whether there are facilities for doing washing/ironing clothes.
Ask whether there is a camp shop/television room/snack bar on the site.
Ask whether you can get take-away food in the area/whether there is a pub in the vicinity with a garden, and how to get there.

13 Problems

You are at a police station in Germany. Your teacher will play the part of the policeman:

- Explain that you have had your bag snatched.
- Wann und wo ist das passiert?
- Say it happened about ten minutes ago in the shopping centre.
- Haben Sie den Täter gesehen?
- Say you had a good look at him/her. Give a detailed description of what he/she looked like and was wearing.

Explain that you have lost/mislaid/can't find your wallet/handbag/camera.
Ask someone whether he/she has seen it anywhere. Say where you think you left it (e.g. in the bus/neighbour's house).
Say that someone has stolen your money/cheque book. Say you are sure it was in your coat pocket/bag/drawer/room, *etc.*
Apologize and explain you have knocked over a cup of coffee/broken a glass. Ask for a cloth/dustpan and brush.
Say the shower/television/telephone/vending-machine doesn't seem to be working.
Ask at a lost property office whether a bunch of keys/leather jacket/pair of gloves/cigarette lighter has been handed in. Give details of the article in question. Say you'll phone/call in tomorrow. Ask about their hours of business.
Go back to a shop/restaurant/café and ask whether you left your camera/coat there.

Role-play cards

Here are ten examples of role-play situations set by various examinations boards in recent years:

---

1 | *Imagine you are in the clothes department of a large German store. Your teacher will play the part of the sales assistant:*

Candidate: Greet the assistant. Ask where the anoraks and coats are.

Examiner: Ich zeige sie Ihnen. Kommen Sie mit!

Candidate: Tell the assistant you are English and ask what size you need.

Examiner: Probieren Sie mal diesen Anorak, Größe 40.

Candidate: Say the anorak he shows you is too big and you don't like the colour.

Examiner: Gefällt Ihnen dieser hier?

Candidate: Say you like the second anorak he shows you and ask how much it costs.

Examiner: Er ist sehr preiswert. Nur DM150.

(LREB)

---

2 | **Man geht schwimmen**

Examiner: Wir gehen heute nachmittag schwimmen, ja?

Candidate: Say that you think it is too cold to go swimming today.

Examiner: Wir gehen nicht ins Freibad sondern ins Hallenbad.

Candidate: Say that you would very much like to go then, and ask what time you will be going.

Examiner: Na ja. Wir essen um halb eins. Wir könnten um halb zwei da sein.

Candidate: Ask if you will be going there by bus.

Examiner: Nein. Mutti geht heute einkaufen. Hoffentlich dürfen wir im Auto mitfahren.

Candidate: Ask how much it costs for an hour's swim.

Examiner: Eine Mark, glaube ich.

(SEREB)

3 | **Bei der deutschen Familie**

Examiner: Guten Morgen. Haben Sie gut geschlafen?
Candidate: Say thank you. You slept very well.
Examiner: Möchten Sie lieber Tee, Kaffee oder Milch?
Candidate: Say you prefer to drink milk at breakfast.
Examiner: Nehmen Sie ein hartgekochtes Ei?
Candidate: Say no thank you. You'll have bread and butter with honey.
Examiner: Hier sind frische Brötchen.
Candidate: Say they taste delicious.
Examiner: Gut. Ich habe sie gerade vom Bäcker abgeholt.

(SEREB)

4 | *You are at the reception desk in a hotel. You want to change some English money. The examiner is the receptionist:*

Examiner: Guten Abend. Kann ich Ihnen helfen?
Candidate: Ask if you can change English money.
Examiner: Jawohl, aber der Kurs hier ist nicht so günstig wie in der Bank.
Candidate: Say the banks are all closed.
Examiner: Wieviel wollen Sie wechseln?
Candidate: Say you will change £10 and ask when the banks open.
Examiner: Um 9.30.

(EAEB)

5 | *You are spending three weeks at a pen-friend's house in Germany. It is the day before you are due to go home. The examiner is your friend's mother/father:*

Examiner: Also (name). Morgen fährst du nach Hause.
Candidate: Ask what you can buy as a present for your parents.
Examiner: Ich würde dir raten, eine kleine Flasche Parfüm für Mutti und vielleicht eine Krawatte für deinen Vater.
Candidate: Ask where you can buy the things suggested.
Examiner: Am besten gehst du mit Franz/Grete in die Stadt.
Candidate: Ask if one can get there by bus.
Examiner: Bestimmt. Der Bus fährt alle fünfzehn Minuten.

(EAEB)

6 *You enter a shop. The shopkeeper says good morning and asks you what you would like:*

Examiner: Good morning. What would you like?
Candidate: Say good morning, and ask for ten eggs.
Examiner: Fine, would you like anything else?
Candidate: Say you would like one hundred grams of liver sausage.
Examiner: Just a moment please. I'll weigh some.
Candidate: Ask for a half a litre of milk as well.
Examiner: So, a carton of milk.
Candidate: Ask if the shopkeeper has a large tin of pears.
Examiner: Yes, would there be anything else?
Candidate: Say no thank you, and ask how much it comes to.
Examiner: Give the amount.

(WMEB)

---

7 *You have just arrived at a pen-friend's house and are chatting with the parents. Your teacher will play the part of one of the parents:*

Examiner: Wie war denn die Überfahrt?
Candidate: Say you have had a good crossing.
Examiner: Und die Strecke mit der Bahn?
Candidate: Tell them the train was very full.
Examiner: Hast du gegessen?
Candidate: Explain that you have not had a meal for several hours.
Examiner: Dann finden wir etwas sofort.
Candidate: Ask at what time you have to get up the following morning.
Examiner: Du kannst morgen ausschlafen.
Candidate: Say you want to send a card home straight away.

(EAEB)

---

8 *You are at a stationer's. Your teacher will play the part of the assistant:*

Examiner: Guten Morgen. Bitte schön?
Candidate: Ask for notepaper and envelopes.
Examiner: Also diese kleine Packung?

Candidate:	Ask how many envelopes there are in the packet.
Examiner:	Je sechs Stück. Die Packung kostet DM1,50.
Candidate:	Ask for a ball-point pen.
Examiner:	Einen billigen, oder etwas Besseres?
Candidate:	Say you want a cheap one. You have left yours at home.
Examiner:	Also zu 25 Pfg. Das macht DM1,75 zusammen.
Candidate:	Say thank you and good-bye.

(EAEB)

9 | *You are passing through the customs. The customs officer asks you a question:*

Examiner:	Have you anything to declare?
Candidate:	Say you have a watch to declare.
Examiner:	Please open your suitcase.
Candidate:	Say you must look for the key.
Examiner:	So, you have two bottles of whisky!
Candidate:	Ask how many bottles you are allowed to take.
Examiner:	Only one; you must pay duty for the other.
Candidate:	Say you will have to change some money.
Examiner:	There's a bank over there on the right.
Candidate:	Thank him, and say you will come straight back.

(WMEB)

10 | *Imagine you arrive at a German youth hostel in the early evening. Your teacher will play the part of the warden:*

Candidate:	Greet the warden. Ask if you can stay for the night.
Examiner:	Ja natürlich, wir haben viele Betten frei.
Candidate:	Ask how much the evening meal costs.
Examiner:	Es ist sehr billig. Nur DM2,50.
Candidate:	Ask if you must pay now or when you leave.
Examiner:	Morgen früh gleich nach dem Frühstück ist mir lieber als jetzt.
Candidate:	Ask how far it is to the next hostel.
Examiner:	Die nächste Jugendherberge befindet sich in Rüdesheim, nur 20 Kilometer von hier entfernt.

(LREB)

Reading comprehension

Points to remember

1 Read the instructions carefully.

2 Read the text carefully, two or three times if necessary.

3 Do not translate the text into English!

4 Answer in full sentences unless you have clear instructions to the contrary.

5 Your answers should be as full as possible; some questions may require several pieces of information. On the other hand, include only information which is relevant to the questions. If in doubt about the relevance of a piece of information, however, it is better to put it in than leave it out!

6 If answers are to be written in German, do not be tempted to copy out chunks of the text. You can be sure that some change in the original words will be necessary. Make sure that the tense and form of your answers suit those of the questions.

7 In short multiple-choice items, work by a process of elimination, rejecting obviously wrong answers and guessing only if you really can't decide between what remains. Don't immediately seize upon an answer which appears correct; always investigate the other alternatives.

Section A

In each of the following sentences a word or phrase is missing. From the four suggested answers, choose the one which makes the best sense:

1 Karl hat seine Brieftasche im Bus liegen lassen. Er geht zum Busbahnhof und geht direkt ......
   a zur Telefonzelle.
   b zur Haltestelle.
   c zum Fahrkartenautomaten.
   d zur Fundstelle.

2 Lisl will sich einen Film im Fernsehen anschauen und will keine Minute davon verpassen. Sie läuft ins Wohnzimmer. Zum Glück hat der Film ...... begonnen.
   a schon lange
   b vor einer Stunde
   c früher am Abend
   d noch nicht

3 Peters Zimmer ist immer in Unordnung. Er macht nie sein Bett, putzt nie seine Schuhe. Er ist ......
   a ein fauler Junge.
   b ein kluger Junge.
   c ein gieriger Junge.
   d ein höflicher Junge.

4 Maria probiert im Kaufhaus eine Jacke an. Ihre Freundin sagt ihr, sie sollte sie kaufen, denn sie findet die Jacke ......
   a schick.
   b häßlich.
   c teuer.
   d scheußlich.

5 Johann freut sich sehr auf den Besuch seines Onkels. Er mag Onkel Willi gern; er sieht ihn aber leider ......
   a oft.
   b selten.
   c regelmäßig.
   d manchmal.

6 Statt zu lernen geht Karin jeden Abend mit der Clique aus. Im Examen fällt sie selbstverständlich durch, denn sie hat ......
   a zu viel gearbeitet.
   b sehr fleißig gearbeitet.
   c nicht genug gearbeitet.
   d stundenlang gearbeitet.

7 Der englische Tourist stellt fest, er hat fast kein deutsches Geld mehr. Er geht also auf die Bank, ...
   a um Geld umzuwechseln.
   b um Geld zu verdienen.
   c um Geld auszugeben.
   d um Geld einzuwerfen.

8 Wie ärgerlich! Herr Braun holt seine Pfeife aus der Tasche. Er kann sie aber nicht rauchen; er hat ...... mitgebracht.
   a sein Feuerzeug
   b viel Tabak
   c ein Päckchen Zigaretten
   d keine Streichhölzer

9 Heute darf man nicht die Bahnhofstraße entlang fahren. Die Straße ist gesperrt und es gibt ......
   a ein Parkhaus.
   b eine Parkuhr.
   c eine Umleitung.
   d einen Zebrastreifen.

10 Auf dem Heimweg muß Frau Schmidt anhalten. Etwas ist mit ihrem Auto nicht in Ordnung. Sie steigt aus und bemerkt sofort, was los ist ......
   a Das Benzin ist alle!
   b Der Kofferraum ist leer!
   c Sie hat ihren Hut vergessen!
   d Sie hat eine Reifenpanne!

11 Herr Meyer hatte neulich einen schweren Autounfall, aber er blieb unverletzt, weil ......
   a das andere Auto völlig kaputt war.
   b er immer vorsichtig fährt.
   c seine Frau am Steuer war.
   d er seinen Sicherheitsgurt anhatte.

(ALSEB)

12 Herr und Frau Koch sind hocherfreut, weil ihre Tochter ihr erstes Baby bekommen hat. Sie haben nämlich jetzt ......
   a einen Schwiegersohn.
   b ein Enkelkind.
   c Großeltern.
   d eine Tochter.

(ALSEB)

Section B

A situation is outlined in German; you are required to find the correct answer to the question in English or choose the phrase which completes the statement in English:

1 Gestern war das Wetter herrlich.
   The weather yesterday was ......
   a dull.
   b overcast.
   c chilly.
   d lovely.

2 Der Zug sollte um halb drei ankommen. Er traf aber endlich mit zwanzig Minuten Verspätung ein.
   The train arrived at ......
   a ten to three.
   b ten to four.
   c twenty past three.
   d half past three.

3 Angela hatte keine Geschwister und ihre Eltern verwöhnten sie. Sie war also ein sehr unangenehmes Kind.
   What sort of a child was Angela?
   a Very nice.
   b Very independent.
   c Very lonely.
   d Very unpleasant.

4 Mutter machte die Tür des Kühlschranks auf.
   Where was mother?
   a In the bedroom.
   b On the landing.
   c In the kitchen.
   d In the lounge.

36

5 An der Grenze mußten die
Reisenden ihre Pässe vorzeigen.
Where had the travellers got to?
  a The border.
  b The airport.
  c The ticket office.
  d The mountain pass.

6 Jede Woche sparte Jürgen
etwas von seinem Taschengeld,
das ihm sein Vater gab.
What did Jürgen do with his
pocket money?
  a He saved some of it.
  b He spent all of it.
  c He gave some to his father.
  d He saved all of it.

(EMREB)

7 Helga ist leider durch ihre
Prüfung gefallen.
Helga ......
  a missed her examination.
  b passed her examination.
  c retook her examination.
  d failed her examination.

8 Als Karl den Brief aufmachte,
war er wütend über das, was er
darin las.
When he read the letter Karl
was ......
  a excited.
  b furious.
  c amused.
  d puzzled.

9 Bevor er nach Deutschland
kam, war Peter nie auf einem
Fahrrad gefahren, aber nach
vier Tagen konnte er
wunderbar fahren.
What happened to Peter in
Germany?
  a He did not dare ride a bicycle.
  b He waited four days before
    riding a bicycle.
  c He rode a bicycle well on the
    first day.
  d He rode a bicycle for the first
    time.

(EMREB)

Section C

A situation is outlined involving one or more persons. You are asked to select
the remark most likely to be made, or the answer most likely to be given, by a
person involved in that situation:

1 Peter ruft Ingrid an, um sie
einzuladen, mit ihm ins Kino
zu gehen. Sie mag ihn und
möchte gern mit ihm ausgehen.
Sie antwortet also:
  a Nichts zu danken!
  b Unmöglich!
  c Einverstanden!
  d Wie schade!

2 Peter hat für seine Prüfung sehr
fleißig gearbeitet; er ist
trotzdem durchgefallen. Er tut
seinem Freund leid. Der Freund
sagt zu ihm:
  a Das war ein Glück!
  b Ich gratuliere!
  c Das hast du verdient!
  d So ein Pech!

3 Herr und Frau Schwarz essen im Restaurant. Sie sind damit unzufrieden, und sehr enttäuscht. Er sagt zu ihr:

a Hier gibt man sich ja viel Mühe!

b Über die Bedienung kann man sich nicht beklagen!

c Wir kommen bestimmt nie wieder hierher!

d Dieses Restaurant empfehle ich allen meinen Freunden!

4 Karin fragt ihre Freundin, um wieviel Uhr die Disko beginnt. Ihre Freundin, die gar nichts von der Disko weiß, antwortet:

a Ich habe keine Ahnung.

b Ich habe keine Uhr.

c Ich habe keine Zeit.

d Ich habe keine Eintrittskarten.

5 Frau Igel sagt zu ihrer Tochter, die gerade mit ihrem Freund tanzen geht:

a Zum Wohl!

b Gesegnete Mahlzeit!

c Grüß Gott!

d Viel Vergnügen!

6 Nach einer Party kommt Willi nach Hause. An seinem Gesicht ist deutlich zu lesen, daß sie nicht so war, wie er hoffte. Er hat offensichtlich schlechte Laune. Seine Mutter fragt, „Wie war's?" Er antwortet:

a Es war wirklich toll.

b Ich habe viel Spaß gehabt.

c Mir hat's gefallen.

d Es war sehr langweilig.

7 Jochen und Erich haben sich seit zwanzig Jahren nicht gesehen. Sie haben sich natürlich viel verändert. Jochen sagt zu Erich:

a Du siehst genauso aus wie früher.

b Wir werden einmal noch älter sein.

c Ich habe dich beinahe nicht erkannt.

d Wir haben uns regelmäßig getroffen.

8 Eine Dame hat gerade einen Artikel im Kaufhaus gekauft. Als sie das Gebäude verläßt, hält sie der Kaufhausdetektiv an und behauptet, sie habe den Artikel gestohlen. Sie kann aber ihre Unschuld beweisen, indem sie sagt:

a Es ist in einer Tüte und der Kassenzettel ist dabei.

b Ich gehe sofort zurück und bezahle es.

c Meine Tasche ist leer; Sie werden nichts darin finden.

d Ich habe den Artikel schon längst zurückgegeben.

9 Frau Bäcker ist fremd in Hamburg. Sie sucht eine Übernachtung. In der Tourist-Informationsstelle empfiehlt man ihr ein gutes, billiges Hotel. Sie sagt:

a Danke für die Rechnung.

b Danke für die Auskunft.

c Danke für die Einladung.

d Danke für die Störung.

10 Der Kellner hat sich in der Rechnung geirrt. Frau Appel ruft ihn herüber und zeigt ihm den Fehler. Er sagt:

a Sie haben recht ... das war dumm von mir!

b Sie haben recht ... das war dumm von Ihnen!

c Seien Sie nicht so dumm ... Kellner machen keine Fehler!

d Was Sie nicht sagen! ... Das ist mir völlig egal!

11 Fräulein Hamm findet das Parfüm, das man ihr im Warenhaus anbietet, viel zu teuer. Sie sagt deshalb zu der Verkäuferin:

a Das kann ich mir nicht leisten.

b Das finde ich spottbillig.

c Das ist wohl ein Sonderangebot.

d Der Preis ist ja günstig.

12 Susi hatte Rainer zu ihrer Party eingeladen. Er mag Parties nicht und ist nicht erschienen. Am folgenden Tag fragt sie ihn, warum er nicht gekommen sei. Er antwortet:

a Ich habe mich gelangweilt.

b Die Party hat nicht stattgefunden.

c Die Party ist ausgefallen.

d Ich hatte keine Lust dazu.

13 Die Ärztin hatte die Patientin untersucht. Dann schrieb sie ein Rezept, gab es ihr und sagte:

a Holen Sie morgen Ihr Rezept ab.

b Hier haben Sie die gewünschte Quittung.

c Gehen Sie damit sofort zur Apotheke.

d Beschreiben Sie mir genau Ihre Symptome.

(SREB)

14 Frau Baum will im Autobus bis zum Bahnhof fahren. Sie fragt den Schaffner:

a Halten Sie auf dem Bahnhofplatz?

b Können Sie schnell fahren? Ich habe es eilig.

c Auf welchem Bahnsteig kommen wir an?

d Wissen Sie, wann der Zug fährt?

(ALSEB)

15 Der kleine Dieter kann nicht schlafen, weil er furchtbare Zahnschmerzen hat. Seine Mutter sagt zu ihm:

a Hast du dir vorm Schlafengehen die Zähne geputzt?

b Morgen gehst du zum Zahnarzt, mein Junge.

c Hast du dich vielleicht erkältet?

d Du hast wohl zu viel zum Abendbrot gegessen.

(ALSEB)

Section D

(i) Pick out the correct meanings of the following signs:

1 | LEBENSMITTEL |

- **a** Lifebelt
- **b** Town centre
- **c** Groceries
- **d** Furniture

2 | BADEVERBOT |

- **a** No bathing
- **b** Boats for hire
- **c** Special offer
- **d** Wash room

3 | BESETZT |

- **a** Open
- **b** Vacant
- **c** Sold out
- **d** Engaged

4 | ZUGAUSKUNFT |

- **a** Train departures
- **b** Train arrivals
- **c** Train information
- **d** Train timetable

(LREB)

5 | FREMDENZIMMER |

- **a** Games room
- **b** Tourist office
- **c** Customs hall
- **d** Accommodation

6 | AUTOVERMIETUNG |

- **a** Car hire
- **b** Second-hand cars
- **c** Car wash
- **d** Car repairs

7 | NOTAUSGANG |

- **a** No exit
- **b** Emergency exit
- **c** Escalator
- **d** Cul-de-sac

8 | RADFAHREN UNTERSAGT |

- **a** Cycle department in basement
- **b** Subway for cyclists
- **c** Path for cyclists
- **d** No cycling

9 | UNFALLSTATION |

- **a** Underground station
- **b** Police station
- **c** Lost property office
- **d** First-aid post

10 | EINFAHRT FREIHALTEN |

- **a** Entrance. Keep clear
- **b** No entry
- **c** Entry free
- **d** Entrance. Stop immediately

(LREB)

40

(ii) The following signs tell you ...

1 | BITTE EINORDNEN |

a to queue up.
b to walk in.
c to get in lane.
d to take one (e.g. leaflet).

2 | BITTE LÄUTEN |

a to ring the bell.
b to wait.
c to be quiet.
d to switch on the light.

3 | EINBAHNSTRASSE |

a the street is called Einbahnstraße.
b it's a tram stop.
c this is the way to the station.
d it's a one-way street.

4 | WARENUMTAUSCH NUR MIT KASSENZETTEL |

a money is only paid out at the cash desk.
b carrier bags are available at the cash desk.
c only cash payments are accepted.
d goods are only exchanged if a receipt is produced.

5 | ACHTUNG DIEBSTAHLGEFAHR |

a to beware of deep water.
b to beware of falling masonry.
c to beware of pickpockets.
d to beware of the sheer drop.

6 | FALSCHPARKER WERDEN KOSTENPFLICHTIG ABGESCHLEPPT |

a those found vandalizing the park will be fined.
b parking is illegal unless a pay disc is displayed.
c cars parked illegally will be towed away at owner's cost.
d unauthorized traffic will be fined.

(LREB)

7 | FÜR SCHWERBEHINDERTE BITTE PLATZ FREIHALTEN |

a Reserved for disabled. Please keep clear.
b Reserved for heavy goods vehicles. Please keep clear.
c Free parking places in the square.
d Free parking for disabled drivers.

(LREB)

(iii) Where would you expect to see the following notices/signs?

1 | ROLLTREPPE |

a In a bus.
b In the street.
c In a department store.
d On a river bank.

2 | BAUSTELLE |

a On the beach.
b At a beauty spot.
c In a lay-by.
d On a building site.

3 | SB-TANKEN | | MÜNZTANK |

a On a boat.
b At a petrol station.
c In a military museum.
d In a campsite shop.

4

a At the swimming baths.
b In a cinema.
c At the station.
d At the airport.

5

a At an hotel.
b At a restaurant.
c At a tobacconist's.
d At a health food shop.

6

a In a pet shop.
b In a safari park.
c In the countryside.
d In a garden centre.

7 | TRIMM-DICH-PFAD |

a In a wood.
b In a hairdresser's.
c In a hardware shop.
d In a launderette.

8 | KARTEN NUR IM VORVERKAUF ERHÄLTLICH |

a In a theatre.
b In a stationer's.
c In a post office.
d At a railway booking office.

(LREB)

(iv) These are advertisements for …

1 **a** travel-sickness pills.
   b indigestion tablets.
   c denture-cleaning tablets.
   d throat tablets.

HalsTeufel haben keine Chance mehr…
Wenn's um den Hals geht
frubienzym
Halsschmerz-Tabletten

2 **a** a German steamer cruise.
   b a car-hire firm.
   c a chain of petrol stations.
   d the German army.

Keine andere Tankstelle in Deutschland trifft man unterwegs so häufig wie die blau-weißen von Aral.
Viele Autofahrer finden das beruhigend.

3 **a** hay fever tablets.
   b vitamin pills.
   c agricultural machinery.
   d eye drops.

Heuschnupfen?
Calcistin
Dragées:
● wirken schnell
● lindern rasch Nieß- und Juckreiz.
Rezeptfrei in Ihrer Apotheke.

4 **a** headache tablets.
   b vacuum cleaners.
   c petrol.
   d a stereo system.

Saugstark wie jeder Siemens-SUPER.
Nur noch feinfühliger.

5
  a air freshener.
  b mouth wash.
  c fly spray.
  d lavatory cleaner.

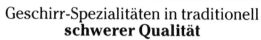

Inspirol
Die Gurgellösung für jeden Tag.

6
  a seeds.
  b cigarettes.
  c crockery.
  d recipe cards.

Geschirr-Spezialitäten in traditionell
schwerer Qualität

Nahrath
Koch-Kultur
. Genuß und sicheres Gelingen

7
  a a driving school.
  b a furniture firm.
  c a motel.
  d motor oil.

MÖBEL
HERTEL

EIN FÜHRENDES EINRICHTUNGSHAUS
OBERFRANKENS

8
  a a vehicle service station.
  b a launderette.
  c an electronics firm.
  d a coach firm.

TÜV-
Hilfe
Hier!
SSS

Bayreuth, Kulmbacher Straße 86
Telefon 09 21/4 18 76

■ Kfz-Meisterbetrieb
■ Autovermietung
■ TÜV-Arbeiten
■ Automatische
  Waschanlage
   ■ Reifen und
    Zubehör

9
a a women's magazine.
b skin moisturizing cream.
c women's hats.
d lipstick.

AN ALLE FRAUEN, DENEN GEGEN TROCKENE HAUT BISHER NICHTS GEHOLFEN HAT.

10
a umbrellas.
b refrigerators.
c beer.
d sunburn cream.

Verdammt, Sonnenbrand . . . . . . **Systral** kühlt und lindert.

11
a kitchens.
b cakes.
c bakeware.
d cookery books.
(LREB)

almaKÜCHEN

Preisgünstig kaufen — direkt beim Hersteller!

alma Küchenzentren in:

NEU: Vorläufig im Verkaufs-Pavillon: **Dortmund-Dorstfeld**

12
a forest camping holidays.
b a timber firm.
c beer stored in the wood.
d hand carving in wood.
(LREB)

FERDINAND REIN

HOLZHANDLUNG

Lager in Laub- und Nadel- schnittholz Sperrholz

HOLZ

5100 Aachen

(v) Look at the following signs, notices, etc. and answer the questions which follow them in the language in which they are asked:

1 a When is parking restricted here and why?

b What restriction on parking is there here?

2 What are these two machines for? What is the difference between them?

3 a

> **Wohnwagen**
> (für 6 Personen) ab Anfang September 1982 zu kaufen gesucht. Angebote unter K 9987 an den Verlag.

> Suche gebrauchtes **Herrenrennrad,** Tel. (09 21) 2 07 13

Do these articles come under 'Articles for sale' or 'Articles wanted'? What are the articles in question?

b

> Junges Ehepaar sucht **3-Zimmer-Wohnung** in Bindlach od. Umgebung. Chiffre-Nr. 114 a. d. NB

> Alleinstehende Dame sucht ab sofort
> **1- bis 2-Zi.-Wohnung**
> mit Küche, Bad, auch Zentrumsnähe Tel. (0921) 57252, von 16–18 Uhr.

Who is looking for what and where?

4

Wien, 1983-06-27

Lieber Österreich-Freund!

Für Ihre Anfrage danken wir herzlich und übersenden Ihnen in der Anlage die gewünschten Informationen. Wir hoffen, daß Sie damit Ihre Urlaubsvorbereitungen treffen können.
Falls Sie weitere Fragen haben, wenden Sie sich bitte an uns. Wir beraten Sie gerne!

Mit freundlichen Grüssen

Ihre
Österreich Information

Where did this letter come from?
What sort of information had been asked for by the person who received it?
What probably accompanied the letter?
What offer is made at the end of the letter?

5

DR. MED. KLAUS HOHLBAUM

Hals - Nasen - Ohrenarzt

Alle Kassen

Sprechzeiten:
Mo., Mi., Fr.   8 - 12 Uhr
Mo., Di., Do., Fr. 15 - 17 Uhr
und nach Vereinbarung

4. Stock   Personenaufzug

An welchem Tag ist der Arzt nur am Vormittag zu sprechen?
An welchen Tagen ist er nur am Nachmittag da?
An welchen Tagen kann man ihn sowohl am Vormittag als auch am Nachmittag besuchen?
An welchen Tagen hat er keine Sprechstunden?

6

SCHLOSS OBERWALD

Eintrittspreise

Erwachsene ....DM 5,00

Kinder u. Jugendliche bis 18 Jahre ....DM 3,50

Reisegruppen ab 20 Pers. ....DM 3,00 pro Pers.

Studenten, Rentner u. Personen ab 60 ....DM 3,50

Herr und Frau Braun besuchen das Schloß. Was müssen sie bezahlen?
Karl ist 19 Jahre alt; er ist aber kein Student. Was bezahlt er?
Herr Schmidt (40 Jahre alt), sein Vater (62 Jahre alt) und sein Sohn (14 Jahre alt) wollen hinein. Was kostet das insgesamt?
30 englische Touristen besuchen das Schloß. Was müssen sie insgesamt bezahlen?

7

EIN FROHES WEIHNACHTSFEST und ALLES GUTE ZUM NEUEN JAHR

Wünscht Dir Dein Neffe — Hans

a In welchem Monat schreibt Hans diese Weihnachtskarte?
Er schreibt sie ......
b Wem schickt er die Weihnachtskarte?
Er schickt ......
c Wo sind die Geschenke?
Sie sind ......
Now answer this question in *one* sentence:
d Was für Weihnachtsgeschenke haben Sie letztes Jahr bekommen?

(EMREB)

8 Look at this section from a Swiss railway timetable.

	D 501	D 503
Basel ab	12.56	14.41
Liestal	13.06	...
Olten an	13.30	15.10
ab	13.32	15.12
Luzern	14.13	15.54

a Wo sind diese Städte?
Sie sind ......
b Wie lange halten die Züge in
Olten? Sie halten ......
c Welcher Zug hält nicht in
Liestal? Der Zug, der ......,
hält nicht in Liestal.
d Was macht D501 um 14.13?

(EMREB)

9 Look at the store guide.

KARSTADT

4.	Stock	Restaurant
		Bank
3.	Stock	Reisebüro
		Sportartikel
2.	Stock	Damenabteilung
		Kosmetik
1.	Stock	Herrenabteilung
		Schallplatten
Erdgeschoss		Schuhe
		Photoartikel

a Wo ist die Herrenabteilung?
Sie ist ......
b Was kauft man vielleicht in der
Sportartikelabteilung? Vielleicht
kauft man ......
c Warum geht man zu einer
Bank? Man geht zu einer Bank,
um ......
Now answer this question in *one*
complete sentence.
d Wie oft gehen Sie einkaufen?

(EMREB)

(vi) Give the gist in English of the following signs, notices and instructions:

1

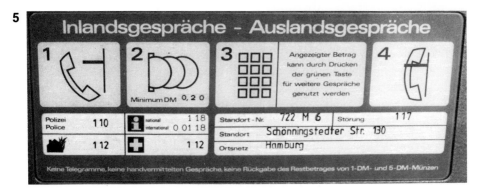

2

Zapfsäule

Motor abschalten!   **Rauchen verboten!**

1. Zapfventil abheben und in Tank einführen.
2. Zapfventil betätigen. Im vollen Tank schließt Zapfventil selbsttätig. Füllgeschwindigkeit kann am Handhebel reguliert werden.
3. Zapfventil bitte sorgfältig einhängen.
4. Tank wieder schließen.
5. Beleg entnehmen und an der Kasse vorlegen.

voir au dos   see on back   vedi al tergo   se baksiden

3
Stellengesuche

Kellner, 28 Jahre, sucht Dauer-stellung in Restaurant oder Caffee mit Schichtarbeit. Angeb. unt. Chiffre-Nr. 117 a. d. NB

Junge Frau sucht **Stellung** in Küche od. Reinigung, ganztags. Chiffre-Nr. 109 a. d. NB, Postf. 110 150

4

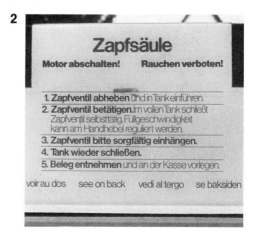

Das Mitbringen v. großen u. kleinen Hunden, das Mitführen von Fahr-rädern, Kinder- und Handwagen **ist streng verboten**

Die Gemeindekirchenräte

5

Inlandsgespräche - Auslandsgespräche

Section E

Read the following passages and answer the questions in the language in which they are written:

1 Giving up smoking

Wenn Sie wirklich mit dem Rauchen aufhören wollen, haben Sie drei verschiedene Möglichkeiten: Sie hören sofort auf; Sie rauchen allmählich immer weniger, bis Sie Nichtraucher sind; Sie rauchen so wenig wie möglich, obwohl es sicher am besten ist, ganz aufzuhören. Um das Aufhören leichter zu machen, können Sie folgendes tun:
- Nehmen Sie nie Streichhölzer, Feuerzeug oder Zigaretten mit.
- Lehnen Sie jede angebotene Zigarette ab.
- Rauchen Sie in bestimmten Situationen nicht, z.B. wenn Sie telefonieren, Tee oder Kaffee trinken, usw.
- Rauchen Sie nur eine halbe Zigarette.
- Rauchen Sie leichte Zigaretten.
- Kaufen Sie erst wieder Zigaretten, wenn die alte Packung leer ist.
- Rauchen Sie nicht vor oder nach Mahlzeiten, denn es ist besonders ungesund.
- Rauchen Sie nicht, wenn Nichtraucher oder Kinder dabei sind.
- Stellen Sie keine Aschenbecher in Arbeits- und Wohnzimmer.
- Schränken Sie das Rauchen auf maximal 10 Zigaretten pro Tag ein.
- Wenn Sie den Wunsch nach einer Zigarette haben, gehen Sie an die frische Luft oder atmen Sie tief vor dem offenen Fenster.

1 What three possibilities are mentioned for those wishing to give up smoking?

2 In your own words, give the gist of the eleven hints for making giving up smoking easier.

2 Zu schnell gefahren

Wegen überhöhter Geschwindigkeit kam das Auto eines 20jährigen aus Pechbrunn, der am Mittwoch gegen 6 Uhr abends von Goldkronach nach Bayreuth fuhr, kurz vor der Allersdorfer Kreuzung auf der nassen Fahrbahn ins Schleudern. Das Auto, das nach rechts geriet und einen Leitpfahl umfuhr, überschlug sich mehrmals und blieb in einem Rübenfeld liegen. Der Autofahrer und sein 20jähriger Beifahrer wurden nur leicht verletzt; sie waren angegurtet.

1 How many men and/or women were involved in the accident?
2 Give two reasons why the accident happened.
3 Give at least three details of what happened.
4 How badly were the people injured and why?

3 Auto gegen Baum

Schwere Verletzungen erlitt ein 66jähriger Autofahrer, der gegen einen Baum geprallt war. Der Mann war am Dienstag vormittag auf der Fahrt von Gefrees nach Hohenknoden vermutlich wegen überhöhter Geschwindigkeit von der Straße abgekommen und am Baum gelandet. Der Schwerverletzte wurde mit dem Rettungshubschrauber nach Bayreuth ins Krankenhaus gebracht. 9000 Mark beträgt der Schaden am Auto, das schrottreif ist.

1 When did the accident happen and where was the driver going to?
2 Where did his car end up?
3 Give two details about the condition of his vehicle.

4 Polizeihund biß zu

Ein Auto, das mit hoher Geschwindigkeit durch die Hofer Straße raste, fiel am Donnerstag um 2 Uhr einer Polizeistreife auf. Sie verfolgte es und konnte es vor dem Maintal-Center stellen. Der Fahrer war inzwischen in eine Diskothek geflüchtet, wo ihn die Beamten ausfindig machten. Als der Mann auf dem Weg zum Streifenwagen erfuhr, daß ihm eine Blutprobe bevorstand, wehrte er sich. Zwei Gäste der Diskothek unterstützten ihn. Die Rangelei verunsicherte den Diensthund so sehr, daß er den 20jährigen und einen der beiden Gäste biß. Als der Fahrer gegen den Hund trat, wurde er ein zweites Mal gebissen. Der Mann konnte, nachdem schließlich Handfesseln angelegt worden waren, zur Blutprobe gebracht werden.

1 Why did the police take special notice of the car in question?
2 What did they do when they saw it?
3 What did the driver do when they stopped him?
4 Why did the driver become violent?
5 Who else became involved in the struggle?
6 Describe how the dog became involved.
7 What finally happened?

5 Die Flucht gelang

14 CSSR-Bürger setzten sich ab – Fünf kamen aus der DDR

14 Touristen aus der CSSR haben sich am Wochenende während einer Besichtigungsfahrt durch Süddeutschland von einer ursprünglich 40köpfigen Reisegruppe abgesetzt. Die Männer und Frauen im Alter von 20 bis 30 Jahren, von denen die meisten aus Prag stammen, benutzten Aufenthalte in Nürnberg, Augsburg und München dazu, um im Westen zu bleiben.

Fünf junge Männer sind aus der DDR in die Bundesrepublik geflohen. Zwei 22jährige Arbeiter schafften es bei Ranbach (Werra-Meißner-Kreis), den Metallgitterzaun, der an dieser Stelle nicht nicht mit Selbstschußanlagen ausgerüstet ist, zu überwinden. Bei Goslar kamen zwei weitere Arbeiter, 22 und 24 Jahre alt, über die Grenze. Der fünfte Flüchtling, ein 29jähriger Soldat der DDR-Grenztruppen in Uniform, setzte sich bei Fulda in die Bundesrepublik ab.

1 Where did the 14 tourists come from?

2 What were they doing in Southern Germany?

3 Why is the number 40 mentioned?

4 What did the 14 do which led to their being featured in this article?

5 Where did the five young men come from?

6 What did the first two manage to do?

7 What happened near Goslar?

8 What do we learn about the fifth man?

6 Einfach ist es nie!

Steward oder Stewardeß sein ist ein Traumberuf für viele junge Leute. Nach einiger Zeit wird natürlich vieles Routine, aber langweilig wird der Job nie. Es ist immer ein großartiges Gefühl, die Erde von oben zu sehen.

Es ist aber nicht leicht Steward bezw. Stewardeß zu werden. Die Kandidaten müssen eine bestimmte Körpergröße und ein bestimmtes Gewicht haben. Dazu müssen sie gepflegt aussehen, kontaktfreudig und ausgeglichen sein. Sie müssen mindestens zwei Fremdsprachen können. Um herauszufinden, ob sich die Kandidaten für den Job eignen, werden sie in mehreren Tests geprüft.

Bei jedem Lufthansa-Flug setzt man die Crew, also die Mannschaft des Flugzeugs, neu aus.

Stewards und Stewardessen arbeiten also ständig mit neuen Kollegen und lernen immer mehr Angestellte der Gesellschaft kennen.

Bevor die Passagiere ins Flugzeug kommen, muß geprüft werden, ob alles für den Notfall bereit steht. Erst dann dürfen sie einsteigen. Sie werden beim Eintreten begrüßt. Dann bekommen sie von den Stewards bezw. Stewardessen Tageszeitungen. Die Stewards und Stewardessen müssen auch darauf achten, daß sich alle Passagiere anschnallen.

Während des Flugs machen Stewards oder Stewardessen die notwendigen Ansagen, beruhigen die Passagiere, die Angst haben, bringen den Fluggästen Speisen und Getränke, und kümmern sich um die Kinder. Das ist ein harter Job. Das Motto lautet: Immer nur lächeln, auch wenn's mal kritisch wird!

(Adapted from *Scala* article.)

1 What is said about the job of being an air steward/hostess?

2 What qualifications are mentioned for becoming one?

3 What are we told about the way Lufthansa crews operate?

4 Eight tasks of an air steward/hostess are mentioned. How many of these can you find?

5 What, according to the passage, is the air steward's/hostess's motto?

7 „Aviophobie"

Sind Sie schon irgendwohin geflogen? Hatten Sie Angst? Ja? Dann befinden Sie sich mit Ihrer Angst in bester Gesellschaft. Die Königin von England, ebenso wie „Großmaul" Muhammad Ali, gehören zu den 75 Prozent der Flugreisenden, die unter der „Aviophobie" (Flugangst) leiden.

Was kann man dagegen unternehmen? Nichts ist sicher aber folgende Tips könnten Ihnen vielleicht helfen:
- Kommen Sie rechtzeitig und gut ausgeschlafen zu Ihrem Flug.
- Wenn Sie eingecheckt haben, bummeln Sie durch den Flughafen. Stimmen Sie sich ohne Hektik auf Ihren Flug ein.
- Meiden Sie kurz vor dem Abflug Kaffee und Alkohol.
- Verscheuchen Sie negative, angstmachende Gedanken durch positives Denken: Auch der Pilot und die Crew wollen wieder heil herunter!
- Lenken Sie sich durch Lesen oder Spiele ab.
- Fangen Sie ein nettes Gespräch mit Ihrem Nachbarn an und gestehen Sie ihm offen Ihre Angst. Das verbindet.

– Wenn der Flug unruhig wird: Ballen Sie fünf Sekunden lang die
Fäuste – dann entspannen. Spannen Sie Ihre Beinmuskeln an – und
entspannen. Atmen Sie ganz tief ein – und locker wieder aus.
– Sagen Sie sich: Alle 30 Sekunden startet oder landet irgendwo auf
der Welt ein Flugzeug. Wir schaffen das auch!

(Adapted from *Bunte* article.)

1 Why are the Queen of England
and Muhammad Ali mentioned?
2 What is 'Aviophobie'?

3 In your own words give the gist of
the hints for combatting it.

8 Es war einmal ein Wald ...

Das Gasthaus „Hanskühnenburg" steht oben auf einem Berg im
Oberharz. Die Herberge ist eins der beliebtesten Wander- und
Ausflugsziele der Gegend. Dort kann der Wanderer, ermüdet vom
langen Aufstieg, unter Hirschgeweihen vor dem Kamin sitzen, sich
ausruhen und einen würzigen Kräuterschnaps trinken und eine
Schüssel selbstgekochte Erbsensuppe genießen.

Kauft man eine Ansichtskarte davon, sieht man die Herberge
zwischen hohen Fichten liegen. Das Foto wurde aber vor elf Jahren
aufgenommen. Heute sieht sie nicht mehr so idyllisch aus. Man sieht
das Wirtshaus schon von weitem, denn der frühere dunkle
Fichtenwald ist total verschwunden! Außer einigen Baumskeletten ist
die Bergkuppe völlig kahl!

Wie ist es dazugekommen? Abgase aus Kraftwerkschloten und
Autoauspuffen bilden mit Luftfeuchtigkeit Säure, die als „saurer
Regen" auf die Wälder fällt und Nadeln und Blätter angreift.
Hinterher zerfressen Käfer die Rinde der kranken Bäume, die bald den
starken Winterwinden nicht mehr widerstehen können.

Im Harz ist es zwar schlimm, aber in vielen anderen Gebieten der
BRD sieht es genauso schlimm aus. Man schätzt, daß rund ein Drittel
aller Wälder in der BRD auf diese Weise stirbt ... und es wird immer
noch schlimmer!

(Adapted from *Stern* magazine.)

1 What is 'Hanskühnenburg' and
what amenities does it offer?
2 What has happened over the
past 11 years?

3 What has been happening to
cause this state of affairs?
4 What is the situation in the
Federal Republic generally?

9 Fragen Sie Frau Martina ...

Liebe Frau Martina!

Seit langem habe ich Probleme mit meinem Vater. Er liest auch einfach meine Briefe. Können Sie bitte deshalb Ihren Rat abdrucken und mir nicht schreiben?

Obwohl ich schon 16 bin, besteht mein Vater immer darauf, daß ich ihm sage, wohin ich gehe, mit wem ich verkehre, und was ich mache. Nun habe ich einen Freund. Meiner Mutter habe ich davon erzählt. Sie hat Verständnis für meine Situation; meinem Vater habe ich nichts darüber gesagt. Gestern hat er uns aber nach der Schule gesehen. Vater hat meine Mutter und mich angeschrien, und gesagt, wir hätten ihn betrogen. Er sagt, er will mich jeden Tag von der Schule abholen, und mir nicht mehr erlauben, abends auszugehen, damit ich meinen Freund nicht mehr treffen kann. Was soll ich nur machen? Was raten Sie mir?

Christina X

Liebe Christina!

Du tust mir leid, denn ich finde, Dein Vater zeigt wenig Verständnis für Dich. Ich bin aber sicher, er meint es gut, und tut das alles nur, weil er Dich liebt, und sich Sorgen um Dich macht. Ich bin der Meinung, er sollte viel mehr Vertrauen zu Dir haben, denn Du bist kein kleines Kind mehr!

Wenn Dein Vater es nicht will, daß Du ausgehst, könntest Du oder Deine Mutter ihm vorschlagen, daß Dein Freund Dich zu Hause besucht. Auf diese Weise kann Dein Vater ihn kennenlernen. Wer weiß, vielleicht findet er, daß er ganz in Ordnung ist!

Frau Martina

1 Why does Christina X particularly request a printed answer rather than a personal letter?

2 What does her father insist on, which she finds unfair on a 16-year-old?

3 What has recently brought matters to a head?

4 What has her father threatened to do?

5 What does Frau Martina think about Christina's father's attitude?

6 What does she suggest that Christina, or her mother, should do?

10 Hitch-hiking

Trampen ist in der BRD grundsätzlich erlaubt. Die Polizei bestraft allenfalls die Autofahrer – wenn sie an der falschen Stelle halten. Auf Autobahnen und ihren Auffahrten darf man nicht halten.

Das Trampen ist nur in der Deutschen Demokratischen Republik und in der UdSSR grundsätzlich verboten.

Eingeschränkt erlaubt ist das Trampen in Schweden, Italien, den Niederlanden und der Schweiz. Die Einschränkung: Man darf nicht auf Hauptverkehrsstraßen trampen, wo man den Verkehr behindern kann, und vor allem nicht auf Autobahnen. In Frankreich dürfen organisierte Gruppen nicht trampen. Problemlos ist es in: Belgien, Bulgarien, Dänemark, Großbritannien, Griechenland, Jugoslawien, Luxemburg, Portugal, Rumänien, Spanien, Tschechoslowakei, Türkei, Ungarn.

Jugendliche unter achtzehn sollten eine schriftliche Erlaubnis ihrer Eltern mitnehmen. Das hilft bei der Polizei.

Bei Unfällen ist man als Tramper am besten dran, wenn der Fahrer eine Insassen-Versicherung hat.

Tips für Tramper
– Mädchen sollten besser nicht allein trampen.
– Beim Einsteigen Wagennummer und Autotyp notieren – damit man der Polizei helfen kann, wenn man Ärger mit dem Fahrer bekommt.
– Paß, Geld usw. nie im großen Gepäck aufbewahren, das im Kofferraum verschwindet – das verschwindet manchmal nämlich für immer.
– Von Rennfahrern sich schnell wieder trennen – sonst liegt man womöglich bald nebeneinander im Krankenhaus.

1 How is hitch-hiking regarded in Germany?
2 Whom do the police punish and for what reason?
3 Where must drivers not stop?
4 In which *two* European countries is hitch-hiking forbidden?
5 In which *four* countries is hitch-hiking restricted?
6 What is the restriction in these countries?
7 Who is not allowed to hitch-hike in France?
8 What should young people under eighteen have on them?
9 What advice is given to female hitch-hikers?
10 What ought the hitch-hiker do when getting into a vehicle?
11 Why?
12 What advice is given about the hitch-hiker's belongings and luggage?
13 From whom is it best to avoid getting a lift? Why?

(NWREB)

11 The Berlin pandas

Die zwei Panda-Bären des Berliner Zoos haben das Herz aller
Zoo-Besucher gewonnen. Der Zoodirektor Dr. Friedrich ist auch mit
ihnen sehr zufrieden. Vor eineinhalb Jahren holte er sie in Peking ab,
und seit sie in dem Zoo sind, kommen zweimal so viele Besucher in
den Zoo wie vorher. Für so populäre Tiere ist bei der Zoodirektion
nichts zu teuer. Das Pandahaus, mit zwei Räumen, Terrasse,
Schwimmbecken und Spielgeräten, hat über 750 000 Mark gekostet.
   Die Tiere zu füttern ist auch ziemlich teuer. Pünktlich um halb
zwei serviert man ihnen eine sorgfältig vorbereitete Suppe: Reis mit
zerschnittenem Grünkohl, Kartoffeln, einem Ei und zwei Eßlöffeln
Honig. Zum Nachtisch bekommen sie rohe Bambusspitzen, aus
Südfrankreich importiert und im Kühlschrank frischgehalten. Dr.
Friedrich sagt: „Schon eine Stunde vor der Fütterung kommen die
ersten Panda-Fans an. Sie wollen einen guten Stehplatz haben, wenn
die Pandas ihre Mahlzeit bekommen."
   Frau Renelt ist auch eine gute Freundin der Pandas. Sie ist
Mieterin des Souvenir-Kiosks am Eingang zum Zoo. „Die
Panda-Artikel sind heute ein Schlager!" sagt sie. Die Kunden kaufen
bei ihr Panda-Puppen, Schlüsselringe, Pandabilder und so weiter. Die
teuersten Andenken sind Silbermedaillen mit einer Abbildung des
Pandapaares, die man an einer Schnur um den Hals hängt.
   In der freien Natur steht es nicht so gut um die lieblichen
Panda-Bären. Nur etwa 1000 von ihnen sind noch in den naßkalten
Bergwäldern des Himalaja zu finden. Dort leben sie von
Bambusspitzen, aber das Futter wird von Jahr zu Jahr knapper, so
daß viele Pandas verhungern.

1 When did the Berlin Zoo first get the pandas?
2 Why is the zoo director pleased with them?
3 What is the attitude of the zoo management to them?
4 Give *three* of the features of the panda house.
5 At what time do the pandas feed?
6 Name *three* of the things that are added to the rice soup.
7 What happens one hour before feeding time?
8 Who is Frau Renelt?
9 Why are the pandas popular with her?
10 Name *three* of the souvenirs mentioned.
11 Describe the most expensive one.
12 What is the natural habitat of the panda?
13 What threatens the future of wild pandas?

(ALSEB)

12 Luxusauto

Über den Rolls-Royce und dessen Besitzer muß es wohl Hunderte von Geschichten und Witze geben. Ich habe keine Ahnung, ob die folgende Geschichte wahr ist, aber ich will sie doch erzählen.

In den sechziger Jahren reiste ein reicher englischer Herr in seinem Rolls-Royce geschäftlich durch die Schweiz. Eines Morgens passierte das Undenkbare – er hatte eine Panne! Zwar war das kein nagelneues Auto – er besaß es schon seit zehn Jahren – aber so was erwartet ein Rolls-Royce-Besitzer nie!

Er ließ das Auto zur nächstliegenden größeren Stadt abschleppen. Obwohl es sich um die größte Reparaturwerkstatt der Stadt handelte, konnte man es nicht sofort reparieren, weil dort die notwendigen Ersatzteile fehlten. Man mußte sich daher mit dem Hauptbüro der Rolls-Royce-Firma in Großbritannien in Verbindung setzen. Per Telegramm kam in wenigen Stunden die Antwort, ein Mechaniker sei unterwegs; man sollte den Besitzer des Autos in dem vornehmsten Hotel der Stadt auf Kosten der Firma unterbringen lassen und ihm ein Auto mit Chauffeur zur Verfügung stellen.

Spät am selben Abend landete ein englischer Mechaniker in Zürich und fuhr direkt zu der Stadt, wo sich das Auto befand. Er machte sich sofort an die Arbeit, arbeitete die Nacht hindurch und war erst in den frühen Morgenstunden mit der Reparatur fertig. Dann fuhr er sofort nach Großbritannien zurück.

Als der Besitzer des Autos am folgenden Morgen von seinem Hotel zur Werkstatt gefahren wurde, fand er sein Auto fahrbereit vor der Werkstatt stehen. Auf seine Frage, was die Reparatur koste, sagte man ihm, er habe nichts zu bezahlen.

Als er von seiner Geschäftsreise nach Hause zurückkehrte, erwartete er, daß bald eine Rechnung oder mindestens ein Brief von der Rolls-Royce-Firma ankommen würde. Sechs Monate vergingen, ohne daß er etwas hörte. Endlich rief er die Firma an. Er nannte seinen Namen, erklärte was passiert war, wann und wo. Nach einigen Minuten kam die Antwort: „Es tut uns leid, wir wissen nicht, wovon Sie reden. Es muß wohl ein Irrtum vorliegen. Uns schulden Sie nichts!"

1 The writer of this text says ......
  a this story is true.
  b he doesn't know whether it's true or not.
  c it's just a joke.
  d he doesn't think it's really true.

2 The man was travelling in ......
  a Sweden.
  b Switzerland.
  c Scotland.
  d Spain.

3 He was there ......
  a on business.
  b on holiday.
  c to visit a firm.
  d to buy an hotel.

4 This incident happened ......
  a ten years ago.
  b last year.
  c in the 1960s.
  d six months ago.

5 The car in question was ......
  a brand new.
  b very old.

c ten years old.
d six years old.

6 The garage couldn't handle the repair ......
  a because they didn't have the necessary spare parts.
  b because the mechanics were out on another job.
  c because the mechanics were inexperienced with this sort of car.
  d because the workshop was too small.

7 What was the gist of the telegram from the Rolls Royce head office?

8 What did the Rolls Royce owner find when he arrived at the garage the next morning?

9 What did he expect when he got home and how long did he wait before phoning the firm?

10 What was the gist of their answer?

13 At a station

Franz Müller sollte am Mittwoch seine Tante in Mainz besuchen. Bei schlechtem Wetter ging er also am Tag vorher in der Mittagspause zum Bahnhof, denn er wollte sich nach den Abfahrtszeiten der Züge und dem Preis der Fahrkarte erkundigen. Als er in die Bahnhofshalle trat, suchte er das Auskunftsbüro. Das fand er gleich an der linken Seite. Nach zehn Minuten war er fertig. Da er erst in einer halben Stunde wieder in der Fabrik sein sollte, beschloß er, noch fünfzehn Minuten dort zu verbringen. Langsam schlenderte er durch die Bahnhofshalle. An der Sperre sah er die Menschen, die mit dem Personenzug aus Limburg gekommen waren. Auf Gleis drei hatte der Eilzug nach Marburg schon lange gestanden. Man holte eine neue Lokomotive.

Am Fahrkartenschalter standen eine junge Dame, die einen kurzen, braunen Mantel und einen gelben Hut trug, und ein Mädchen. Ein Mann, der am Schalter vorbeiging, hatte zwei Koffer und schob sie auf einem Kuli. Er hatte es eilig. Mit den schweren Koffern war er ganz atemlos, als er den Zug nach Marburg erreichte. Franz sah auch die vielen Geschäfte, und dachte: „Morgen kaufe ich hier Pralinen für meine Tante".

Endlich stand er wieder an der Eingangstür. Das Wetter war jetzt ganz anders, und er konnte den Regenmantel ausziehen. Als er wieder auf dem Weg zur Arbeit war, begegnete er einem Kollegen, dem es in letzter Zeit nicht gut gegangen war, und zusammen eilten sie zur Fabrik.

1 When did Franz Müller go to the station?
  a On Tuesday.
  b On Wednesday.
  c On Thursday.
  d On Friday.

2 Why did he go?
  a To meet his aunt.
  b To buy some tickets.
  c To check on train times.
  d To have lunch.

3 How long did he spend at the station?
  a 10 minutes.
  b 15 minutes.
  c 25 minutes.
  d 30 minutes.

4 Which train had just arrived?
  a A local train.
  b An express train.
  c The train to Marburg.
  d The train to Limburg.

5 What was the young lady wearing?
  a A long coat.
  b A short coat.
  c A green coat.
  d A yellow coat.

6 Which man went past the ticket office?
  a A man carrying two cases.
  b A man carrying three cases.
  c A man who had come out of a shop.
  d A man pushing a trolley.

7 What are we told about him?
  a He was early for his train.
  b He was walking slowly.
  c He was going to platform two.
  d He was out of breath.

8 What did Franz intend to buy?
  a Flowers.
  b Chocolates.
  c Fruit.
  d Magazines.

9 What was the weather like as he left the station?
  a Wetter than before.
  b Colder than before.
  c Drier than before.
  d The same as before.

10 Which colleague did he meet?
a One who was usually last to work.
b One who had not been well.
c One who had been to the station.
d One who worked well.

(EMREB)

14 Herr Dutz saß am Frühstückstisch, aß ein Käsebrot und blätterte die „Fernsehwoche" durch, um sich die besten Programme für den Abend auszusuchen. Plötzlich bemerkte er die Worte „Großes Preisrätsel! Ein VW zu gewinnen!" Herr Dutz hatte schon einen Mercedes, aber seine Frau wollte auch einen Wagen haben. Deshalb las Herr Dutz weiter. Im September würde das Fernsehen jeden Abend ein Bild von einer Großstadt zeigen; wer alle Städte nennen könnte, würde den Preis gewinnen. Herr Dutz war Auslandsagent für seine Firma und mit Hilfe einiger Landkarten erkannte er ohne große Schwierigkeiten alle dreißig Städte. Dann schickte er seine Liste ab und wartete.

Als das Resultat erschien, sah er, daß er alle Städte richtig genannt hatte. Aber am folgenden Tag bekam er einen Brief von der Zeitschrift mit einem Scheck über DM200. Nicht nur Herr Dutz, sondern noch achthundertsiebenundsechzig andere Leser hatten die Städte erkannt, und er mußte den Wert des VW mit allen diesen teilen.

1 Herr Dutz ......
a las die Tageszeitung.
b sah ein Fernsehprogramm.
c blätterte die Abendzeitung durch.
d frühstückte.

2 Um einen VW zu gewinnen, mußte man ......
a viele Städte kennen.
b ein Mercedesfahrer sein.
c eine große Reise machen.
d im Ausland wohnen.

3 Im September ......
a hatte Herr Dutz Schwierigkeiten mit dem Fernseher.
b sah Herr Dutz täglich fern.
c schickte Herr Dutz viele Karten.
d wartete Herr Dutz auf eine Karte.

4 Wieviele andere Leute hatten den Preis gewonnen?
a 876.
b 877.
c 867.
d 868.

(WMEB)

15 Thefts from holiday-makers: tricks of the trade

„Wer wurde im Urlaub 1981 bestohlen?" fragte der Deutsche Automobilklub seine Mitglieder und bekam zur Antwort mehr als 400 Briefe. Damit auch andere Touristen, die bisher glücklich davongekommen sind, von den schlimmen Erfahrungen der Bestohlenen profitieren können, machte der Automobilklub auf die beliebtesten Tricks der Urlaubsgangster aufmerksam.

Als allererstes muß man wissen, daß die Diebe ihr Opfer manchmal mehrere Tage lang beobachten, um auf den Augenblick zu warten, in dem sie ungestört an die Arbeit gehen können. Das erfuhr Walther Rau, der mit seiner Familie in einem Badeort an der spanischen Küste Urlaub machte. Er war schon von Freunden und durch Zeitungsartikel vor der Urlaubskriminalität in Spanien gewarnt worden und nahm alle Mahnungen ernst. Während der ganzen Ferien ließ er das Auto nie allein und hatte alle Wertsachen – Geld, Reiseschecks, Reisepässe und die paar Schmucksachen, die seine Frau mitgebracht hatte, – in dem Hotelsafe in Sicherheit gebracht. So hatte er seine Ferien ohne Sorge genießen können – bis zum letzten Tag.

Am Tag der Heimreise nach Deutschland lud die Familie das ganze Gepäck in das Auto ein. Weil das Wasser so lockend aussah und weil es ihnen beim Packen des Autos so richtig warm geworden war, beschlossen sie, ein letztes Mal zu baden. Sie parkten das Auto auf dem harten Sand, wo sie es im Auge behalten konnten, zogen sich schnell das Badezeug an, legten die Kleider ins Auto auf die Sitze, verschlossen sorgfältig Fenster, Türen und Kofferraum und sprangen ins Meer.

Die beiden Eltern waren mit ihren Kindern – einem sechzehnjährigen Sohn und der anderthalb Jahre jüngeren Tochter – etwa hundert Meter hinausgeschwommen, als der Sohn dem Vater zurief, ein fremder Wagen habe neben ihrem Wagen eingeparkt. Und dann mußte die Familie hilflos mit ansehen, wie innerhalb weniger Sekunden Türen und Kofferraum ihres Autos mit einer Eisenstange aufgebrochen wurden, der ganze Inhalt blitzschnell in das andere Auto umgeladen wurde und die Diebe sich ebenso flink davonmachten wie sie gekommen waren.

Bis der Vater das Ufer wieder erreichte, waren gut fünf Minuten vergangen. Er mußte feststellen, daß nicht nur das ganze Gepäck, sondern auch der Rest des Urlaubsgeldes, der für die Heimreise bestimmt war, und auch die Kleider, die sie vor dem Baden ausgezogen hatten, verschwunden waren. An eine Verfolgung der

Diebe war auch nicht zu denken, denn diese hatten auch noch einen Vorderreifen aufgeschlitzt.

Kein Wunder, daß Herr Rau seinen Brief an den Automobilklub mit den Worten beendete: „Nie wieder nach Spanien!"

1 Why did the German Automobile Club publish their report?

2 What is the first lesson to be learnt?

3 How did Walther Rau know about the risk of theft before he went on holiday in Spain?

4 What precautions did he take whilst on holiday?

5 Why did the family decide to have one last swim before leaving for home?

6 Where did they park the car before this swim?

7 What measures did they take against thieves before going into the water?

8 What did the son call out to his father when the family was swimming?

9 How did the thieves go to work?

10 How long did the robbery take?

11 What had the family lost?

12 Why was it not possible to pursue the thieves?

(WJEC)

Listening comprehension

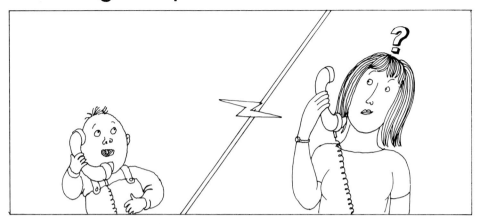

Points to remember

1 Where you are required to write your own answers to questions, include all relevant matter, but try to include only that which is relevant. If you are not sure whether to include something, it is better to put it in than to omit it!

2 In short multiple choice items it is a good idea to eliminate any options which seem obviously wrong and concentrate on the 'possibles'. If you really cannot decide between any of the remaining ones, you'll have to go by the 'feel' of the answer (i.e. guess!). Never leave a question unanswered. If you give no answer you definitely lose a mark. With a guess you have a one in four chance of gaining a mark.

3 If one of the options strikes you immediately as right, look at the alternatives just the same. You may have been cleverly 'distracted'! Check to see that the alternatives are obviously wrong. If you then have any doubts, think again.

4 Listen to the whole item. Don't seize upon a single noun or verb and jump to a conclusion. Tense and context are very important. For example you may be asked where the speakers are, and hear something about '...... schwimmen ......'. You could be excused for assuming that they are on the beach or at a swimming pool. If you listen more carefully, you may hear 'Es ist zu kalt, um schwimmenzugehen. Ich bleibe zu Hause ...' etc. You might hear something about '...... Supermarkt ......' and assume that the speakers are in a supermarket. In fact, the speaker could be saying 'Ich war gestern im Supermarkt' or 'Ich bin auf dem Weg zum Supermarkt'.

5 Don't panic! It is better to guess an item than to dwell on it and get flustered.

Section A

In this section you will hear a number of short conversations. You will hear each conversation twice. You are to identify who the speakers are:

1 a A tourist and his wife.
  b A customs officer and a tourist.
  c A shop assistant and a customer.
  d A porter and a passenger.

2 a A shop assistant and a customer.
  b A rock singer and a fan.
  c A young man and his girlfriend.
  d A young man and a passer-by.

3 a A teenager and his sister.
  b A teacher and a girl pupil.
  c A father and his daughter.
  d A headmaster and a young teacher.

4 a A farmer and a farmhand.
  b A bank clerk and a customer.
  c A taxi driver and a fare.
  d A greengrocer and a customer.

5 a Ein Apotheker und sein Kunde.
  b Ein Automechaniker und sein Kunde.
  c Ein Polizist und ein Autofahrer.
  d Ein Kaufhausdetektiv und ein Taschendieb.

6 a Ein Tourist und ein Taxifahrer.
  b Ein Tourist und ein Gepäckträger.
  c Ein Tourist und ein Busfahrer.
  d Ein Tourist und ein Flughafenangestellter.

7 a Eine Frau und eine Zahnärztin.
  b Eine Frau und eine Sprechstundenhilfe.

c Eine Frau und eine Tierärztin.
d Eine Frau und eine Apothekerin.

8 a Ein Mann und eine Vorbeigehende.
  b Ein Mann und eine Taxifahrerin.
  c Ein Mann und die Empfangsdame im Hotel.
  d Ein Mann und eine Angestellte des Verkehrsvereins.

9 a Ein LKW-Fahrer und ein Tramper.
  b Ein Schwimmbadangestellter und ein Kunde.
  c Ein Student und sein Vater.
  d Ein Eisenbahnschaffner und ein Reisender.

10 a Ein Buchhändler und sein Kunde.
   b Ein Kellner und sein Kunde.
   c Ein Metzger und sein Kunde.
   d Ein Blumenhändler und sein Kunde.

11 a Ein Bankdirektor.
   b Ein Briefmarkensammler.
   c Ein Postbeamter.
   d Ein Kassierer.

(SREB)

12 a Ein Busfahrer.
   b Ein Schalterbeamter.
   c Ein Bahnhofsvorsteher.
   d Ein Schaffner.

(SREB)

66

Section B

In this section you will hear some short conversations. You will hear each one twice. You are to identify what the speakers are doing or where they are:

1 a They are walking past a cathedral.
b They are driving past a cathedral.
c They are planning a visit to a cathedral.
d They are at a bus stop opposite the cathedral.

2 a They have just finished washing up.
b They are just about to get petrol.
c They are about to leave for the theatre.
d They are just parking the car.

3 a They are watching television.
b They are in the cinema.
c They are looking at the newspaper.
d They are watching a tennis match.

4 a They are sitting in a boat.
b They are on the beach.
c They are taking photographs.
d They are looking at photographs.

5 a Sie verbringen den Tag am Strand.
b Sie machen Pläne für den folgenden Tag.
c Sie babysitten für ihre Eltern.
d Sie erzählen sich Witze.

6 a Sie sind auf dem Weg zur Schule.
b Sie sind gerade heimgekommen.

c Sie sind in ihrem Büro.
d Sie sind im Restaurant.

7 a Sie sind auf der Straße.
b Sie sind in einer Konditorei.
c Sie sind vor dem Kino.
d Sie sind vor einem Parkhochhaus.

8 a Sie sind im Badezimmer.
b Sie sind am Hoteleingang.
c Sie sind am Strand.
d Sie sind im Hallenbad.

9 a Sie sind im Zoo.
b Sie sind im Garten.
c Sie sind beim Gemüsehändler.
d Sie sind in der Küche.

10 a Sie besteigen einen Berg.
b Sie schlagen ein Zelt auf.
c Sie kaufen sich Sportkleidung.
d Sie bringen ein Segelboot ins Wasser.

11 a Sie essen zu Hause zu Mittag.
b Sie gehen auf die Bank.
c Sie halten sich an einem Rastplatz auf.
d Sie kaufen Möbel für ihr neues Haus.

12 a Auf dem Tennisplatz.
b Im Sportgeschäft.
c Auf dem Sportplatz.
d Im Turnverein. (SREB)

13 a Auf dem Bahnhof.
b Im Büro.
c An der Bushaltestelle.
d Im Wartesaal. (SREB)

Section C

In this section you will hear a series of short statements or passages. You will hear each one twice. Answer the questions in English:

1 Where does Karl live?

2 Where does Christina live?

3 Where must Frau Dölz go and why?

4 What happened about the football match and why?

5 Where does Herr Hamm go and why?

6 Where is David going? When? For how long?

7 What mood are the children in and why?

8 What do the Brauns feel about their son and why?

9 Where are the Schmidts planning on going and what must be done first?

10 Where does Frau Winkler's son live and why can't she visit him?

11 Where does Anton's mother think his football socks are? (Give as much detail as possible.)

(EAEB)

12 What was the first event for the school party, and where did it take place?

(EAEB)

Section D

In this section you will hear a series of short statements or passages. You will hear each one twice. Choose the correct answer to the questions from those suggested:

1 What is the speaker saying?
  a He's inviting someone to a party on Saturday evening.
  b He likes going to Saturday night parties.
  c He's giving a party on Saturday evening.
  d He's looking forward to a party on Saturday evening.

2 What did Karin do after she had bought the dress?
  a She took it back to the shop.
  b She ordered another one.
  c She told everyone about it.
  d She tried it on straight away.

3 What is the lady saying to her daughter?
  a She's telling her she should go out in the sunshine.
  b She's telling her she should put some warm clothes on.
  c She's offering her some freshly baked cakes.
  d She's telling her she should go back in the water.

4 When will Herr Gruber be in?
  a Tomorrow afternoon.
  b Tomorrow morning.
  c This morning.
  d In two days' time.

5 What does it say in the newspaper about Margit Mühlhof?
  a She has got married recently.
  b She's had a baby recently.
  c She has died recently.
  d She has had an accident recently.

6 What was Petra's phone message?
  a She's not coming because she's ill.
  b She's been called into work urgently.
  c She's just bought a new car and wants to show it to them.
  d She needs a tow to a garage.

7 Who visited whom?
  a Karl visited his grandparents this weekend.
  b Karl's grandparents came to see him last weekend.
  c Karl's grandparents visited him this weekend.
  d Karl visited his grandparents both weekends.

8 What is the girl suggesting to her friend?
  a That they go over to another counter.
  b That they go down to the next floor.
  c That they go up to the next floor.
  d That they go to another store.

9 Why was Fräulein Bäcker late for work today?
  a Because she was held up in the traffic.
  b Because she overslept.
  c Because she had a fall.
  d Because her car broke down.

10 What does the girl decide to do?
  a To go for a walk in town.
  b To go swimming.
  c To go to the pictures.
  d To play miniature golf.

11 What was the class's attitude?
  a They liked the English teacher.
  b They liked the Mathematics teacher.
  c They hated the English teacher.
  d They didn't like the English teacher.

(EMREB)

12 Where will the speaker sleep?
  a By the window.
  b In a room on his own.
  c In his own room.
  d In a large room.

(EMREB)

69

Section E

There now follows a series of texts and dialogues. You will hear each of them twice. Answer the questions (in the appropriate language), giving all the relevant details.

1

1 What is the person receiving the instructions looking for?
2 Give the gist of the instructions for finding it.

2

1 What is the person being spoken to looking for?
2 Where does her friend suggest she should go?

3

1 Where is this person getting directions to?
2 Give the gist of the directions.

4

1 How frequent are guided tours of the caves?
2 How long do they last?
3 When is the next one due to start?
4 What is not permitted in the caves?
5 What five things are mentioned as being available at the kiosk?
6 Where is the kiosk situated?

5

1 What time is it when the man makes this announcement?
2 When will the group be setting off again?
3 What does the man ask the pupils to do and why?
4 Where are the toilets?

6

1 What have these people come to see?
2 How much too early have they arrived?
3 When does the place open?
4 What three suggestions does the guide make for killing time until the place opens?

7

a 1 What sort of train is being announced and where is it coming from?
2 When is it due to arrive at, and leave, this station?
3 How late is it?

b 4 What is the number of the train being announced?
5 Where is it from and where is it going to?
6 What time is it due to arrive at this station?
7 Which platform will it be arriving at?

c 8 Which platform is mentioned in this announcement?
9 What sort of a train is being announced and where is it from?
10 When is it due to arrive at this station?
11 What information concerns first-class passengers?
12 Where is the restaurant car?

70

13 How long is it due to wait at this station?

14 Where is it going to?

15 What should passengers note about this particular train?

8

a 1 What flight is being called and where is it going?

2 Where are the passengers for this flight to go?

3 Why is 10.40 mentioned?

b 4 How many details can you understand of this announcement about a flight from London?

9

1 What information is there of interest to anyone travelling towards Hamm?

2 What can drivers travelling to the Netherlands expect and what has caused it?

3 What is facing drivers to Kassel on the Bundesstraße 6?

4 What is the situation for drivers to Austria on the Munich–Salzburg motorway?

5 What is said about traffic in all other areas?

6 What weather conditions can be expected?

10

1 What day and date is this weather forecast for?

2 What situation does the satellite picture show?

3 What weather can be expected in the morning and how will it change by midday?

4 What will the evening weather be like in the South of the country?

5 And in the North?

6 What maximum daytime temperatures can be expected in these two regions?

11

1 What are the first two items on the programme at eight o'clock?

2 What sort of film is it that Curd Jürgens stars in with Maria Schell?

3 At what time does it start?

4 What is the documentary film about?

5 When does it start and what detail is given about it?

6 What can be seen at 10.30?

7 What are the final two items on the evening's programme?

8 What time is transmission due to end?

12 Diebe!

1 How old is Winifred?

2 Where does she live and how long has she lived there?

3 What do we learn about her husband and other relatives?

4 What is her financial situation?

5 For whom does she always buy presents?

6 What do we learn about these presents?

7 How does she manage to afford them?

8 When did this incident take place?

9 How much money had she had, and where had she kept it?

10 Describe in detail how the two boys stole the money.

11 What were the police able, or not able, to do?

12 What was the 'happy ending' to the story?

13 Ein Tag an der See

a 1 In what season did this story take place?

2 Where did he take the food from?

3 What did he prepare for his lunch?

4 Where did he put the food?

5 Why would he need to take some money?

b 6 At what time did he arrive at the seaside?

7 Where did he go first?

8 How do you know that he was hot?

9 What happened to his ice-cream?

c 10 What had he remembered to bring?

11 Why could he not eat his lunch?

d 12 Why had everyone left the beach?

13 What was he thinking about on the return journey?

14 What was his final piece of bad luck?

(SEREB)

14 The ski fanatic

Part 1

1 What is Marlene's hobby?

2 When did Marlene see the notice about the trip?

3 How long was the trip to last?

4 Name *two* articles she took with her.

5 Where did she put the articles?

6 What was the date of her departure?

7 How long had she been looking forward to the holiday?

Part 2

8 What was Marlene wearing the day after she arrived?

9 What could she see all around her?

10 When did the ski lesson begin?

11 For how long did she practise?

12 When did the accident take place?

13 What injury did she receive?

14 What will she do next year, and why?

(WMEB)

15 Elternsprechtag

1 Who are Frau Schneider and Herr Dickmann?

2 What is the occasion of their meeting?

3 What particular problems has Erika got?

4 What could happen to her if things continue in this way?

5 Why has Frau Schneider had little time to help her?

6 What has Erika often been failing to do?

7 What chance does Herr Dickmann see of Erika's getting over these problems and why?

8 What two things does Frau Schneider say she'll do in future?

16 In der Reparaturwerkstatt

1 What does the customer first say about his car?

2 Why does the garage man say the customer is lucky?

3 Why would it be difficult for the customer to be without his car for long?

4 What initial observations and diagnoses does the garage man make?

5 What does he say about the likely cost?

6 What does he say he'd do if he found more serious problems?

7 What time can the car be picked up and what is important about this particular time?

8 What does the customer intend to do in the meantime?

17

1 Why did Hans particularly want to go to the football match?
  a Because all his friends were going.
  b It was a cup game.
  c Because his favourite team Hamburg was playing.
  d To avoid visiting his grandmother.

2 Why had Hans' mother arranged to visit his grandmother?
  a To celebrate the grandmother's sixtieth birthday.

  b As it was Hans' sixteenth birthday.
  c To give the grandmother a coffee pot.
  d As the grandmother was ill.

3 When will they have coffee?
  a At two o'clock.
  b At 3.30 p.m.
  c At four o'clock.
  d At 4.30 p.m.

4 Why had Hans not yet bought a present for his grandmother?
  a He found it difficult to buy something for someone who had everything she needed.
  b He had no money.
  c He had forgotten to buy her something.
  d He didn't want to buy her anything.

5 What did Hans' mother suggest he buy?
  a Some writing paper.
  b A rose bush.
  c A pink handkerchief.
  d A few roses.

(LREB)

18 A bank robbery

1 The witness had seen ......
  a just the beginning of the incident.
  b very little of the incident.
  c just the end of the incident.
  d the whole of the incident.

2 The witness had just left ......
  a the bank.
  b a cake shop.
  c a grocer's shop.
  d a hardware shop.

3 How many men were involved in the robbery altogether?
  a Two. **c** Four.
  b Three. **d** Five.

4 The get-away car was ......
  a waiting opposite the bank.
  b waiting down the road.
  c waiting around the corner.
  d being driven around the block.

5 The witness ......
  a heard the alarm bell.
  b heard two screams.
  c heard lots of shouting.
  d heard two gun shots.

6 The police were called by ......
  a the witness.
  b the bank manager.
  c a bank employee.
  d a passer-by.

7 The witness told the police ......
  a the colour of the get-away car.
  b no details about the get-away car.
  c the number of the get-away car.
  d the make of the get-away car.

8 The detective asked the witness to come to the police station ......
  a to speak to his superior.
  b to look at some photographs.
  c to arrange an interview.
  d to sign the statement.

19 An einem Samstag

1 Was machen Peter und Ulrike um 12 Uhr?

  a Sie gehen zur Schule.
  b Sie erholen sich vom Wochenende.
  c Sie machen sich auf den Weg nach Hause.
  d Sie überlegen, wo die Straßenbahn hält.

2 Was wollen Sie am Abend machen?
  a Ins Kino gehen.
  b Travolta besuchen.
  c Zu Hause bleiben.
  d Fußball spielen.

3 Was macht Peter, nachdem er sich verabschiedet hat?
  a Er steigt in die Straßenbahn ein.
  b Er begleitet Ulrike nach Hause.
  c Er fährt allein nach Hause.
  d Er geht langsam heim.

4 Warum ärgert sich Peter am Abend?
  a Weil zwei Straßenbahnen an ihm vorbeifahren.
  b Weil seine Freundin so lange warten muß.
  c Weil Ulrike nicht pünktlich kommt.
  d Weil die Straßenbahn Verspätung hat.

5 Warum sind die beiden vor dem Kino enttäuscht?
  a Weil sie rechtzeitig gekommen sind.
  b Weil sie keine Karten mehr bekommen.
  c Weil sie 20 Minuten vor der Kasse stehen müssen.
  d Weil sie sich beeilen müssen.

(SREB)

74

Listening comprehension
Teacher's section

Section A
Each item is recorded twice.

1 — Ich habe ihm doch gesagt, wir
hätten nichts zu verzollen.
— Er muß aber mindestens ein paar
Koffer kontrollieren, Liebling.
— Warum ausgerechnet unsere aber
... das möchte ich gerne wissen!!

a A tourist and his wife.
b A customs officer and a tourist.
c A shop assistant and a
customer.
d A porter and a passenger.

2 — Schau mal! Da ist ein schöner
Rock.
— Er würde mir aber sehr schlecht
stehen.
— Quatsch! Er würde gut zu deiner
Bluse passen.
— Hast du aber den Preis gesehen?
Einfach lächerlich!

a A shop assistant and a
customer.
b A rock singer and a fan.
c A young man and his girl friend.
d A young man and a passer-by.

3 — Warum hast du deine Hausauf-
gaben nicht gemacht?
— Ich mußte auf meine jüngeren
Geschwister aufpassen.
— Das ist doch wohl keine aus-
reichende Entschuldigung!

a A teenager and his sister.
b A teacher and a girl pupil.
c A father and his daughter.
d A headmaster and a young
teacher.

4 — Bitte schön. Was darf es sein?
— Ich hätte gerne zwei Pfund Äpfel.
— Bitte sehr. Wollen Sie eine
Einkaufstüte?
— Nein danke. Ich glaube es geht
auch so.

a A farmer and a farmhand.
b A bank clerk and a customer.
c A taxi driver and a fare.
d A greengrocer and a customer.

5 — Sie wissen, warum ich Sie
angehalten habe?
— Nein. Mir ist nicht bewußt, daß
ich etwas falsch gemacht hätte.
— Sie sind zu schnell gefahren. Ich
muß Ihnen daher einen Strafzettel
ausstellen.
— Ach du meine Güte! Ich habe gar
nicht auf die Geschwindigkeit
geachtet!

a Ein Apotheker und sein Kunde.
b Ein Automechaniker und sein
Kunde.
c Ein Polizist und ein Autofahrer.
d Ein Kaufhausdetektiv und ein
Taschendieb.

6 — Könnten Sie mich bitte zum
Flughafen fahren?
— Ja sicher ... Ist das Ihr Gepäck?
— Ja ... Ich habe es aber sehr eilig!
— Steigen Sie ein! Das schaffen wir
bestimmt in einer Viertelstunde.

a Ein Tourist und ein Taxifahrer.
b Ein Tourist und ein
Gepäckträger.
c Ein Tourist und ein Busfahrer.
d Ein Tourist und ein
Flughafenangestellter.

7 — Ich benötige die Arznei sehr
    dringend.
— Haben Sie ein Rezept Ihres Arztes
    dabei?
— Nein, das habe ich dummerweise
    vergessen!
— Es tut mir leid. Die Arznei ist
    rezeptpflichtig. Ich darf sie Ihnen
    nicht ohne Rezept aushändigen.

a Eine Frau und eine Zahnärztin.
b Eine Frau und eine
    Sprechstundenhilfe.
c Eine Frau und eine Tierärztin.
d Eine Frau und eine Apothekerin.

8 — Ich suche ein Einzelzimmer mit
    Dusche.
— Wo soll das Hotel denn liegen?
— Ziemlich zentral.
— Ich rufe zunächst das Hotel Adler
    an. Es liegt in der Stadtmitte.
    Dort haben wir vielleicht Glück
    ...

a Ein Mann und eine
    Vorbeigehende.
b Ein Mann und eine Taxifahrerin.
c Ein Mann und die
    Empfangsdame im Hotel.
d Ein Mann und eine Angestellte
    des Verkehrvereins.

9 — Hallo! Wohin wollen Sie denn?
— Nach Bad Wimpfen.
— Ich fahre nicht direkt über Bad
    Wimpfen ... Kann Sie aber bis
    Heilbronn bringen, wenn Sie
    wollen.
— Prima!
— Steigen Sie mal ein!

a Ein LKW-Fahrer und ein
    Tramper.
b Ein Schwimmbadangestellter und
    ein Kunde.
c Ein Student und sein Vater.
d Ein Eisenbahnschaffner und ein
    Reisender.

10 — Haben Sie etwas ausgesucht,
    meine Herrschaften?
— Die Vorspeise haben wir schon
    gewählt. Welches Hauptgericht
    können Sie empfehlen?
— Forelle mit Mandeln kann ich
    Ihnen besonders empfehlen. Das
    ist unsere Hausspezialität.

a Ein Buchhändler und sein
    Kunde.
b Ein Kellner und sein Kunde.
c Ein Metzger und sein Kunde.
d Ein Fischhändler und sein
    Kunde.

11 — So, hier sind Ihre Marken ...
    Zehn zu fünfzig Pfennig und fünf
    zu sechzig. Die Wohlfahrtsmarken
    bekommen wir erst morgen
    wieder. Das Päckchen nach
    Amerika geben Sie bei meinem
    Kollegen am Schalter drei ab.

a Ein Bankdirektor.
b Ein Briefmarkensammler.
c Ein Postbeamter.
d Ein Kassierer.

                         (SREB)

12 — Was! Sie haben keine Fahrkarte.
    Von Hamburg nach Stuttgart
    ohne Fahrkarte zu fahren ist ja
    unerhört! So etwas gibt es nicht.
    Sie müssen den doppelten
    Fahrpreis bezahlen oder am
    nächsten Bahnhof aussteigen.

a Ein Busfahrer.
b Ein Schalterbeamter.
c Ein Bahnhofsvorsteher.
d Ein Schaffner.

                         (SREB)

Section B

Each item is recorded twice.

1 — Ein bißchen langsamer, Herbert,
damit der Andrew einen guten
Blick auf den Dom bekommt.
Schade, daß man hier nicht
anhalten darf.

a They are walking past a
cathedral.
b They are driving past a
cathedral.
c They are planning a visit to the
cathedral.
d They are at a bus stop opposite
the cathedral.

2 — Wir müssen bloß noch das
Geschirr spülen. Dann können
wir sofort fahren. Ich habe
nämlich schon getankt.
— Schön. Aber wir müssen uns
trotzdem beeilen. Das Theater
beginnt in 20 Minuten, und es ist
immer schwer, einen Parkplatz au
finden.

a They have just finished washing
up.
b They are just about to get petrol.
c They are about to leave for the
theatre.
d They are just parking the car.

3 — So einen blöden Film habe ich in
meinem Leben noch nicht
gesehen. Wollen wir nicht lieber
etwas im Radio hören?
— Sei mal ruhig! Der Film ist gleich
zu Ende. Dann kommt deine
Lieblingssendung ... Sport.

a They are watching television.
b They are in the cinema.
c They are looking at the
newspaper.
d They are watching a tennis
match.

4 — Dieses Bild von dir am Strand ist
sehr schön geworden. Wer hat es
eigentlich geknipst?
— Ich glaube Jürgen. Aber du, schau
mal her! Dieses Bild von uns
beiden im Ruderboot gefällt mir
prima!

a They are sitting in a boat.
b They are on the beach.
c They are taking photographs.
d They are looking at photographs.

5 — Kommst du morgen früh mit zum
Strand? Wenn es heiß ist, können
wir baden gehen.
— Vormittags gern! Denn später
muß ich bestimmt wieder auf
meine Geschwister aufpassen.

a Sie verbringen den Tag am
Strand.
b Sie machen Pläne für den
folgenden Tag.
c Sie babysitten für ihre Eltern.
d Sie erzählen sich Witze.

6 — Ich habe immer großen Appetit,
wenn ich den ganzen Morgen im
Büro gearbeitet habe.
— Komischerweise habe ich zu
Hause oder in der Schule nie
Hunger. Aber sobald ich wie jetzt
eine Speisekarte in die Hand
kriege, werde ich sofort hungrig.

a Sie sind auf dem Weg zur
Schule.
b Sie sind gerade heimgekommen.
c Sie sind in ihrem Büro.
d Sie sind im Restaurant.

7 — Hier dürfen Sie nicht parken.
Aber am Ende der Straße befindet
sich ein großes Parkhaus. Es ist
direkt neben dem Kino.
— Das ist ja ärgerlich. Ich wollte
bloß schnell eine Torte in diesem
Geschäft kaufen.

a Sie sind auf der Straße.
b Sie sind in einer Konditorei.
c Sie sind vor dem Kino.
d Sie sind vor einem Parkhochhaus.

8 — Ich kann mein Badetuch nicht finden. Habe ich es vielleicht im Hotelzimmer liegenlassen?
— Nein, du hast es wahrscheinlich im Auto gelassen. Oder es liegt hier hinter dir im Sand.

a Sie sind im Badezimmer.
b Sie sind am Hoteleingang.
c Sie sind am Strand.
d Sie sind im Hallenbad.

9 — Die wilden Kaninchen fressen den ganzen Kohl auf, den ich hier angepflanzt habe.
— Schade. Du hast ja so hart gearbeitet. Für den Kochtopf haben wir dieses Jahr leider sehr wenig.

a Sie sind im Zoo.
b Sie sind im Garten.
c Sie sind beim Gemüsehändler.
d Sie sind in der Küche.

10 — Hier wird es steil! Jetzt geht's nur mit dem Seil weiter.
— Der Gipfel ist aber deutlich zu sehen.
— Gut, daß ich neue Stiefel gekauft habe. Mit den Trainingschuhen hätte ich es nie geschafft!

a Sie besteigen einen Berg.
b Sie schlagen ein Zelt auf.
c Sie kaufen sich Sportkleidung.
d Sie bringen ein Segelboot ins Wasser.

11 — Da drüben sind Tische und Bänke. Setzt euch hin, Kinder!
— Wir müssen schnell machen. In mindestens zehn Minuten möchte ich wieder unterwegs sein.

a Sie essen zu Hause zu Mittag.
b Sie gehen auf die Bank.
c Sie halten sich an einem Rastplatz auf.
d Sie kaufen Möbel für ihr neues Haus.

12 — Packen Sie mir bitte einen Ball, ein Netz und einen Tischtennis-schläger ein.
— Gern, Frau Müller. Und wie wäre es mit einem guten Turnhemd?

a Auf dem Tennisplatz.
b Im Sportgeschäft.
c Auf dem Sportplatz.
d Im Turnverein.

(SREB)

13 — Fährst du immer mit dem Bus nach Hause oder nimmst du manchmal den Zug?
— Da diese Haltestelle näher bei dem Büro liegt als der Bahnhof, warte ich lieber hier.

a Auf dem Bahnhof.
b Im Büro.
c An der Bushaltestelle.
d Im Wartesaal.

(SREB)

Section C

Each item is recorded twice.

1 Karl wohnt mitten auf dem Lande auf einem Bauernhof.

Where does Karl live?

2 Christina wohnt bei ihren Großeltern in der Großstadt.

Where does Christina live?

3 Frau Dölz muß zum Zahnarzt, denn ihr ist eine Plombe 'rausgefallen.

Where must Frau Dölz go and why?

4 Das Fußballspiel mußte ausfallen, weil drei von den Spielern auf dem Weg zum Stadion einen Autounfall hatten.

What happened about the football match and why?

5 Da er seine Brille in der Straßenbahn liegenließ, geht Herr Hamm zum Fundbüro, um danach zu fragen.

Where does Herr Hamm go and why?

6 Anfang Juli fährt David nach Österreich, um drei Wochen bei seinem Brieffreund zu verbringen.

Where is David going? When? For how long?

7 Die Kinder freuen sich. Das Wetter ist so heiß, daß sie heute hitzefrei haben. Keine Schule also!

What mood are the children in and why?

8 Die Brauns sind sehr stolz auf ihren Sohn. Er hat gerade das Abitur bestanden und geht bald auf die Uni.

What do the Brauns feel about their son and why?

9 Bevor die Schmidts ins Ausland fahren, müssen sie sich eine Autokarte besorgen und Plätze auf der Fähre buchen lassen.

Where are the Schmidts planning on going and what must be done first?

10 Frau Winkler möchte ihren Sohn in den Vereinigten Staaten besuchen. Das ist aber nicht möglich, denn lange Seereisen mag sie nicht, und sie hat große Angst vorm Fliegen.

Where does Frau Winkler's son live and why can't she visit him?

11 „Mutti, wo sind meine Fußballsocken, bitte?" ruft Anton. „Ich glaube, sie sind entweder in einer Schublade oder oben auf dem Kleiderschrank in deinem Zimmer," antwortet seine Mutter.

Where does Anton's mother think his football socks are? (Give as much detail as possible.)

(EAEB)

12 Eine deutsche Schulgruppe kam um zehn Uhr in unserer Stadt an. Kurz danach wurden die Kinder von dem Bürgermeister im Rathaus begrüßt.

What was the first event for the German school party, and where did it take place?

(EAEB)

Section D

Each item is recorded twice.

1 Ich freue mich auf die Party am Samstagabend.

What is the speaker saying?
a He's inviting someone to a party on Saturday evening.
b He likes going to Saturday night parties.
c He's giving a party on Saturday evening.
d He's looking forward to the party on Saturday evening.

2 Karin kaufte sich ein Kleid. Etwas war damit nicht in Ordnung. Sie ging zum Laden zurück und reklamierte es.

What did Karin do after she had bought the dress?
a She took it back to the shop.
b She ordered another one.
c She told everyone about it.
d She tried it on straight away.

3 Möchtest du einen probieren? Ich habe sie gerade gebacken. Sie sind noch schön warm.

What is the lady saying to her daughter?
a She's telling her she should go out in the sunshine.
b She's telling her she should put some warm clothes on.
c She's offering her some freshly baked cakes.
d She's telling her she should go back in the water.

4 Leider ist Herr Gruber weder heute noch morgen früh im Büro. Wenn Sie aber morgen Nachmittag wiederkommen würden ...

When will Herr Gruber be in?
a Tomorrow afternoon.
b Tomorrow morning.
c This morning.
d In two days time.

5 Es steht hier in der Zeitung, die Margit Mühlhof hat gerade geheiratet.

What does it say in the newspaper about Margit Mühlhof?
a She's got married recently.
b She's had a baby recently.
c She's died recently.
d She had an accident recently.

6 Petra hat gerade angerufen. Sie hat eine Panne und sagt, wir sollten ihr Auto zur Werkstatt abschleppen.

What was Petra's phone message?
a She's not coming because she's ill.
b She's been called into work urgently.
c She's just bought a new car and wants to show it to them.
d She needs a tow to a garage.

7 Voriges Wochenende war Karl zu Besuch bei seinen Großeltern. Dieses Wochenende waren sie es, die ihn besuchten.

Who visited whom?
a Karl visited his grandparents this weekend.
b Karl's grandparents came to see him last weekend.
c Karl's grandparents visited him this weekend.
d Karl visited his grandparents both weekends.

8 Hier im Erdgeschoß gibt's nichts Besonderes. Gehen wir hinauf in den ersten Stock gucken, was es dort gibt.

What is the girl suggesting to her friend?
a That they go over to another counter.
b That they go down to the next floor.
c That they go up to the next floor.
d That they go to another store.

9 Heute kommt Fräulein Bäcker zu spät ins Büro. Nicht wegen des Verkehrs, was oft der Fall ist, sondern weil sie verschlafen hat.

Why was Fräulein Bäcker late for work today?
a Because she was held up in the traffic.
b Because she overslept.
c Because she had a fall.
d Because her car broke down.

10 Es ist zu kalt, um schwimmenzugehen. Der Minigolfplatz ist zu, und ich habe kein Geld, um ins Kino zu gehen. Es gibt also nur noch eins ... einen Stadtbummel machen!

What does the girl decide to do?
a To go for a walk in town.

b To go swimming.
c To go to the pictures.
d To play miniature golf.

11 Die Klasse hatte den Englischlehrer gern, aber den Mathematiklehrer konnte sie nicht leiden.

What was the class's attitude?
a They liked the English teacher.
b They liked the Mathematics teacher.
c They hated the English teacher.

d They didn't like the English teacher.

(EMREB)

12 Dein Bett ist am Fenster in meinem großen Schlafzimmer, und ich schlafe allein im kleinen Nebenzimmer.

Where will the speaker sleep?
a By the window.
b In a room on his own.
c In his own room.
d In a large room.

(EMREB)

Section E

Each passage is recorded once, but should be played twice.

1 „Biegen Sie an der nächsten Kreuzung links ab. Nach etwa 100 Metern finden Sie das Warenhaus ‚Hertie' an der rechten Seite der Straße, dem Kino gegenüber. Sie können es nicht verfehlen."

2 „Wenn du ein Geschenk für deinen Bruder suchst, findest du bestimmt etwas im dritten Stock, denn dort haben sie eine große Spielwarenabteilung ..."

3 „Na ja ... das Einkaufszentrum ist ziemlich weit von hier. Sie können nicht zu Fuß dorthin gehen. Nehmen Sie lieber die Straßenbahn. Die Linie 12 bringt Sie zum Marktplatz ... Steigen Sie dort aus! Vom Marktplatz aus ist es ein Katzensprung ..."

4 „Meine Damen und Herren! Führungen durch die Tropfsteinhöhlen finden alle Dreiviertelstunden statt. Der Aufenthalt in den Höhlen dauert etwa fünfundzwanzig Minuten. Die nächste Führung beginnt in zehn Minuten. Das Fotografieren innerhalb der Höhlen ist nicht gestattet. Dias und Ansichtskarten, sowie Andenken, Süßwaren und Getränke sind am Kiosk beim Höhleneingang erhältlich."

5 „Hört mal zu Kinder! Wir rasten hier. Es ist jetzt kurz vor elf Uhr. Wir machen uns in genau einer halben Stunde wieder auf den Weg ... Das heißt um halb zwölf ... Ich wiederhole: Abfahrt um halb zwölf. Ich bitte euch: keine Minute später! Und noch eine Bitte ... Nehmt alles mit, was ihr braucht! Der Bus wird verschlossen. Ihr könnt also Fotoapparate und andere Wertsachen ruhig hier im Bus lassen. Die Toiletten befinden sich hinter dem Gebäude ... OK? Bis bald also ..."

6 „Da sind wir also, meine Damen und Herren – Schloß Greifenstein. Wir sind ein bißchen früher angekommen als erwartet. Das Schloß macht nachmittags erst um zwei Uhr auf. Wir haben also etwa 40 Minuten totzuschlagen. Sie können ruhig im

Bus warten, oder – was ich Ihnen empfehle – Sie können im Café um die Ecke einen Kaffee trinken. Ein Spaziergang durch den Schloßgarten ist auch die Mühe wert. Er ist sehr schön um diese Jahreszeit und ist durchgehend geöffnet."

7 a „Achtung, Achtung! Der Nahverkehrszug aus Ulm, planmäßige Ankunft 14.30, planmäßige Abfahrt 14.36, hat voraussichtlich 25 Minuten Verspätung. Ich wiederhole ..."

b „Der Zug Nummer D312 von Frankfurt nach Hamburg-Altona, planmäßige Ankunft in Hamburg-Hauptbahnhof um 20.30 Uhr fährt heute auf Gleis drei ein. Ich wiederhole ..."

c „Achtung, bitte, am Gleis acht! Der verspätete Intercity ‚Walküre' aus Bayreuth läuft in wenigen Minuten ein. Die Wagen der Ersten Klasse befinden sich im mittleren Teil des Zuges. Der Speisewagen befindet sich am Schluß des Zuges. Dieser Zug fährt nach kurzem Aufenthalt weiter nach Frankfurt am Main. Der Zug ist zuschlagpflichtig. Bitte Vorsicht bei der Einfahrt des Zuges. Ich wiederhole ..."

8 a „Lufthansa-Flug A795! Alle Passagiere des Lufthansa-Flugs A795 nach London werden gebeten, sich am Ausgang C33 einzufinden; letzte Abfertigung ist um 10.40."

b „Achtung! Achtung! Wegen dichten Nebels über Heathrow hat der British Airways Flug B436 aus London, planmäßige Ankunftzeit 10.20, voraussichtlich 25 Minuten Verspätung ..."

9 „Hier ist der Verkehrslagebericht im gemeinsamen Nachtprogramm der ARD. Auf der E1 zwischen den Anschlußstellen Münster-Süd und Hamm-Nord kommt es nach einem schweren Verkehrsunfall zu erheblichen Verkehrsbehinderungen auf der Fahrbahn in Richtung Hamm ...

... An den Grenzübergängen Aachen und Venlo muß in Richtung Niederlande mit längerem Verkehrsstau gerechnet werden infolge des Bummelstreiks der niederländischen Zöllner ...

... Auf der Bundesstraße 6 von Marburg nach Kassel hat sich ein schwerer Auffahrunfall ereignet. Die Spur in Richtung Kassel ist für einige Zeit gesperrt. Bitte folgen Sie den Umleitungshinweisen der Polizei ...

... Auf der Autobahn München – Salzburg kommt der Verkehr zum Teil nur zähflüssig vorwärts. An der Grenze wird ein Stau von drei Kilometern gemeldet ...

... Im übrigen Bundesgebiet fließt der Verkehr störungsfrei. Im gesamten Bundesgebiet kommt es in den Morgenstunden zu Nebelbildung und teilweise sehr geringer Sichtweite. Auf Brücken und in Flußniederungen besteht Gefahr von Glatteisbildung. Wir bitten die Autofahrer, vorsichtig zu fahren."

10 „Es folgt nun der Wetterbericht für Montag, den 26. April. Unser Satellitenbild zeigt Wolken über den meisten Gebieten der Bundesrepublik. Nach anfänglichem Regen in vielen Gebieten wird sich das Wetter aber gegen Mittag aufklären. Gegen Abend werden dann die starken zum Teil stürmischen Nord- bis Nordwestwinde für den Norden eine neue Regenfront mit zum Teil gewittrigen Schauern bringen, während der Süden weitgehend sonnig bleiben wird. Tageshöchsttemperaturen werden im Süden 20 bis 23°C und im Norden 18°C sein. Ich wünsche Ihnen einen guten Abend."

11 „Guten Abend, liebe Zuschauer. Ich möchte Ihnen nun einen Überblick über unser Programm für den heutigen Sonntagabend geben: Wie immer werden wir um 20 Uhr mit der Tagesschau und dem Wetterbericht beginnen. Um 20.15 Uhr folgt dann eine weitere Folge der Tatortserie. Kommissar Müller wird heute Abend einen besonders mysteriösen Mord untersuchen. In den Hauptrollen können Sie Curd Jürgens und Maria Schell sehen ... Um 21.45 Uhr werden wir einen Dokumentarfilm über Indien zeigen. Dieser Film hat deutsche Untertitel ... Danach können Sie um 22.30 Uhr die heutige Ausgabe der Sportschau mit den neuesten Fußballergebnissen sehen. Wir werden unser Programm mit den Nachrichten um 23.30 Uhr und anschließender Ziehung der Lottozahlen beenden. Sendeschluß wird voraussichtlich gegen 0.05 Uhr sein. Ich wünsche Ihnen gute Unterhaltung."

12 Diebe!

Mrs Winifred White, eine geborene Londonerin, hat ihr ganzes Leben lang in der englischen Hauptstadt gelebt. Sie ist jetzt 72 Jahre alt. Ihr Mann ist längst tot und die einzigen Verwandten, die sie hat, sind ihre Tochter, ihr Schwiegersohn und deren zwei Kinder. Ihr könnt euch vorstellen, wie sehr sie diese beiden Enkelkinder liebt.

Obwohl sie Rentnerin ist, und deswegen sehr wenig Geld bekommt, kauft sie immer für diese Kinder schöne, teure Geburtstags- und Weihnachtsgeschenke. Dafür muß sie natürlich monatelang sparen.

Kurz vor Weihnachten vorigen Jahres hatte sie £25 für ihre Weihnachtsgeschenke. Seit dem Geburtstag ihres Enkelsohnes im Juli hatte sie etwa £1 pro Woche gespart. Dann passierte etwas Schreckliches; das Geld wurde gestohlen.

Eines Morgens klopfte es an der Tür. Sie machte auf und sah einen Jungen vor der Tür, der sie höflich um Erlaubnis bat, sein Modellflugzeug in ihrem Hintergarten zu suchen. Sie hatte natürlich nichts dagegen; sie ging sogar mit, um ihm beim Suchen zu helfen. Das Flugzeug wurde schnell gefunden. Der Junge bedankte sich und lief davon. Als sie aber zurück ins Wohnzimmer trat, war die Schublade, in der sie das Geld aufbewahrte, offen. Das Geld war weg! Ein anderer Junge war ins Haus gekommen, während sie im Garten waren und hatte das Geld genommen. Die Polizei konnte weder die Jungen noch das Geld auftreiben. Die Sache hatte aber ein unerwartetes Happy-end, denn einige von Winifreds Nachbarn, die in der Zeitung von dem Diebstahl gelesen hatten, legten zusammen und brachten die gestohlenen £25 auf. Sie konnte schließlich doch die Geschenke kaufen.

13 Ein Tag an der See

a Herr Schmidt hatte immer Pech. Eines Frühlingmorgens beschloß er, an die See zu fahren. Es war der erste warme Tag des Jahres nach einem langen, kalten Winter. Er nahm Butter und Käse aus dem Kühlschrank, machte sich Käsebrote und legte sie mit Obst und Tomaten in einen Korb. Aber wo war sein Portemonnaie? Geld würde er brauchen, um Benzin zu kaufen.

b Um Viertel vor neun war er unterwegs, und eine Stunde später war er da. Zuerst machte er einen Spaziergang in die Stadtmitte, ehe er zum Strand ging. Er kaufte ein Eis, und weil es ihm warm war, legte es auf eine Bank und zog seine Jacke aus. In diesem Augenblick lief ein Hund darauf zu und fraß es.

c Herr Schmidt hatte eine Badehose mitgebracht, und er ging schwimmen. Nachher aber entdeckte er, daß er vergessen hatte, ein Handtuch mitzubringen. Er setzte sich auf den Sand und erinnerte sich dann, daß sein Mittagessen noch auf dem Tisch in der Küche stand! Bald schlief er ein.

d Als er aufwachte, war kein Mensch mehr da; es regnete in Strömen! Er lief zum Auto zurück. Er freute sich auf ein warmes Bad und sein bequemes Bett. Als er aber endlich vor seiner Haustür stand, konnte er den Hausschlüssel nicht finden!

(SEREB)

14 The ski fanatic

Part 1

Marlene treibt sehr gern Sport. Letztes Jahr fuhr sie mit einer Schulgruppe nach Süddeutschland, um an einem Skikurs teilzunehmen. Anfang November hatte sie eine Notiz am Schwarzen Brett gesehen. Die Skitour sollte länger als eine Woche dauern. Die Fahrt war nicht teuer, aber sie mußte etwas Taschengeld mitbringen. Schon zwei Tage vor der Abfahrt packte sie ihre Skisachen in den Koffer: Skihosen, Skistiefel und eine Schneebrille.

Am siebzehnten Februar stieg sie mit ihren Schulkameraden in den Zug ein. „Seit drei Monaten freue ich mich auf diesen Tag," sagte sie. Endlich erreichte sie ihr Reiseziel: Garmisch-Partenkirchen.

Part 2

Am folgenden Tage stand Marlene vor der Skihütte. Sie trug einen roten Trainingsanzug und sah sehr eifrig und ungeduldig aus. Sie bewunderte die schöne Landschaft. Ringsum sah sie nur schneebedeckte Berge. Kurz nach Sonnenaufgang begann der Skikurs. Der Skilehrer zeigte ihr, wie sie die Stöcke halten sollte. Danach übte sie zwei Stunden lang. Am Ende war sie atemlos. Ganz erschöpft ging sie zur Hütte zurück.

Acht Tage später konnte sie die Ubungshügel blitzschnell auf Skiern hinunterfahren. Doch am Tage vor der Rückfahrt ist sie leider hingefallen. Ihr linker Arm war gebrochen. Sie mußte sofort ins Krankenhaus.

„Trotzdem werde ich nächstes Jahr wieder Skilaufen, weil es mir großen Spaß macht," sagte sie.

(WMEB)

15 Elternsprechtag

— Guten Tag, Frau Schneider. Sie sind also die Mutter von Erika?
— Guten Tag, Herr Dickmann. Sie sind wohl Erikas Klassenlehrer?
— Ja, liebe Frau Schneider. Es ist gut, daß Sie zum Elternsprechtag kommen. Ihre Tochter hat nämlich einige Probleme mit Mathematik und Geschichte.
— Ja, das weiß ich. Sie hat das heute beim Frühstück erwähnt.
— Sie wissen ja, daß man mit zwei Fünfen im Zeugnis die Klasse wiederholen muß. Diese Gefahr besteht leider bei Ihrer Tochter.
— Was kann ich denn machen? Sie wissen, wenn man berufstätig ist, dann bleibt

nicht viel Zeit, um den Kindern bei den Schulaufgaben zu helfen.
— Ja, die Schulaufgaben sind wohl das Problem. Erika ist nämlich nicht dumm,
aber sie erscheint häufig ohne Hausaufgaben. Mit etwas mehr Fleiß müßte sie es
eigentlich schaffen.
— Ich werde mal ein ernstes Wort mit ihr reden. Vielleicht nehme ich mir in
Zukunft auch Zeit, ihre Hausaufgaben abends zu kontrollieren.
— Das wäre sehr gut, denn wir Lehrer brauchen die Mitarbeit der Eltern.
— Gut, daß Sie mir dies alles mitteilen, Herr Dickmann. Schönen Dank und auf
Wiedersehen.

16 In der Reparaturwerkstatt

— Guten Morgen! Ich hatte heute früh große Schwierigkeiten, mein Auto zu
starten. Könnten Sie wohl mal nachschauen, was damit los ist?
— Ja, Sie haben großes Glück. Wir haben gerade etwas Zeit, um das sofort zu tun.
Normalerweise müssen Sie sich bei uns vorher anmelden.
— Wissen Sie, ich fahre jeden Tag mit dem Wagen, und es wäre schwierig für
mich, wenn er längere Zeit ausfiele. Aber wenn Sie jetzt Zeit haben, ist ja alles
in Ordnung.
— Die Batterie ist noch intakt, denn Sie sagen ja, daß alle Lichter beim
Startvorgang aufleuchten. Ich vermute, daß mit der Zündung etwas nicht in
Ordnung ist.
— Wird die Reparatur sehr teuer sein?
— Nein, ich denke nicht. Die Kosten werden unter DM 250 liegen. Wenn es andere
Probleme geben sollte, würden wir vorher Ihr Einverständnis für die Reparatur
einholen. Sie stehen ja im Telefonbuch?
— Ja, Berger ist mein Name, Klaus Berger. Wann kann ich den Wagen dann heute
wieder abholen?
— Sagen wir so gegen sechs Uhr. Kommen Sie aber bitte nicht später, denn dann
treffen Sie niemanden mehr in der Werkstatt an.
— Gut! Dann ist also jetzt alles klar. Ich gehe zum Einkaufen in die Stadt und
schaue dann gegen sechs wieder vorbei.
— In Ordnung. Dann wird der Wagen auch sicher fertig sein.

17 *Hans:* Mutti, darf ich am Samstagnachmittag mit Rudi zum Fußballspiel gehen?
Die Kölner spielen für den Pokal gegen Duisburg.

Mutti: Am Samstag? Nein, das geht nicht. Wir müssen Oma besuchen. Samstag ist
ihr sechzigster Geburtstag. Ich habe ihr gesagt, daß wir um vier Uhr zum
Kaffee bei ihr sein werden. Sie wird sehr enttäuscht sein, wenn du nicht
mitkommst. Übrigens, hast du ihr schon ein Geburtstagsgeschenk gekauft?

Hans: Nein. Ich habe keine Ahnung, was ich ihr schenken soll. Sie scheint doch
alles zu haben, was sie braucht.

Mutti: Kauf ihr ein paar Blumen. Du weißt, sie hat Rosen gern.

(LREB)

18 A bank robbery

— Sie haben also den Überfall gesehen? Könnte ich Ihnen einige Fragen stellen?
— Ich stehe Ihnen gerne zur Verfügung, Herr Kommissar. Ich habe alles von
  Anfang an gesehen.
— Gut, dann erzählen Sie mal, wie das passiert ist.
— Ich kam aus der Konditorei gegenüber der Bank, als ich zwei Männer eilig in die
  Bank gehen sah.
— Was war mit dem Fluchtauto? Haben Sie das auch von Anfang an bemerkt?
— Ja, das kam mir gleich seltsam vor, daß ein Auto mit laufendem Motor um die
  Ecke wartete, an dessen Steuer ein dritter Mann saß.
— Was haben Sie also gemacht?
— Ich wußte nicht, ob ich den Alarm geben sollte oder ob ich besser alles
  beobachten sollte, um nachher als Zeugin dienen zu können.
— Gut, was passierte dann weiter?
— Nach kurzer Zeit rannten die zwei Männer aus der Bank, und das Auto fuhr
  blitzschnell vor, so daß sie einsteigen konnten.
— Haben Sie Schüsse gehört?
— Ja, zweimal war ein Knall zu hören.
— Was haben Sie gemerkt, als das Fluchtauto losfuhr?
— Ich bin schnell in die Bank gelaufen, um zu sehen, was passiert war.
— Haben Sie dann die Polizei verständigt?
— Nein, das hatte bereits einer der Bankangestellten getan, als ich hereinkam.
— Konnten Sie sich die Nummer des Fluchtautos merken?
— Leider nicht, Herr Kommissar ... die Marke auch nicht. Ich sah nur, daß es
  dunkelrot war.
— Wahrscheinlich war es gestohlen. Kommen Sie doch jetzt bitte mit aufs
  Präsidium. Ich werde dort Ihre Aussage tippen lassen und brauche dann nur
  noch Ihre Unterschrift.
— Ja, ich komme gern mit, Herr Kommissar.

19 An einem Samstag

Um 12 Uhr ist die Schule aus und das Wochenende kann beginnen. Ulrike und ihr
Freund Peter gehen zur Straßenbahnhaltestelle und überlegen, was sie am Abend
unternehmen wollen. „Du, Peter," sagt Ulrike „Ich möchte den neuen Travolta-Film
sehen." Peter will sich eigentlich an dem Abend ein Fußballspiel im Fernsehen
anschauen aber er ist einverstanden. Sie verabschieden sich. Ulrike steigt in ihre
Straßenbahn ein, während Peter zu Fuß nach Hause geht.

Um acht Uhr abends wartet Peter an der Haltestelle. Zwei Straßenbahnen fahren
an ihm vorbei, aber in keiner sitzt Ulrike! Peter ist schon böse, daß er so lange auf
sie warten muß. Erst nach zwanzig Minuten kommt sie mit der dritten Straßenbahn
an. „Nach dem Abendessen mußte ich alles abwaschen," erklärt sie. Sie eilen zum
Kino aber alle Plätze sind leider ausverkauft. Was tun? Plötzlich hat Ulrike eine
Idee. „Statt Travolta im Kino zu sehen, können wir zu seinen Platten in einer Disko
tanzen, ja?"

(SREB)

Talking and writing about pictures

Answering questions on pictures: Points to remember

1 Consider each question carefully and decide exactly what is being asked. No credit is given for good German which does not answer the question!

2 In answer to questions involving **wer? was?** make sure you answer using a noun in the same case as that of the question word:
i.e. **wer?/was?** – nominative
wen?/was? – accusative
wessen? – genitive
wem? mit wem? womit? etc. – dative

3 Be careful to answer in the same tense as that of the question.

4 Answer in complete sentences unless there are specific instructions to the contrary.

5 The following notes on how to answer certain types of question, although by no means exhaustive, will be useful:
wo? – where? → preposition (**in/auf/an/neben/vor**, etc.) + dative
wohin? – where (to)? →|**zu** + dative; **in/auf/an/neben/vor**, etc. + accusative
|**nach** + name of town/country, etc.
woher? – where from? → **aus** + dative; **von** + dative
warum? – why? →|, **um** ...... **zu** + infinitive
|, **weil** ...... + verb
wozu? – for what reason, purpose? →|, **um** ...... **zu** + infinitive
|, **damit** ...... + verb
wie? – how? →|adverb (**blitzschnell, sehr laut**, etc.)
|adverbial phrase (**mit einem Schlüssel**, etc.)
|, **indem** ...... + verb

wann? – when? → **um** + clock time
am + part of day (**Vormittag**, etc.)
im + season/month
am + calendar date/day of the week

Note the following questions carefully:
Wie ist ......? – *What is ...... like?*
Wie sieht ...... aus? – *What does ...... look like?*
Was für ein(e)(n) etc. ......? – *What sort of ......?*
Wie spät ist es? – *What is the time?*

Questions on pictures: Practice

Study the pictures and then answer in German the questions beneath them:

1 Wer kommt gerade an, und wie sind sie angekommen?
2 Wo ist der Mann, der rechts auf dem Bild steht, und was macht er gerade?
3 Warum sieht die Frau überrascht aus?
4 Was sagt die Frau wohl zu Ihrem Mann?
5 Was werden sie wohl zu ihren Gästen sagen, wenn sie eintreten?

1 Wie spät ist es, und wie ist das Wetter?
2 Wo kommt diese Familie her, und warum ist sie wohl in Deutschland?
3 Wen sieht man sonst auf dem Bild?
4 Warum sieht der Vater so besorgt aus?
5 Was machen die Mutter und das Kind?

3

1 Wieviele Leute sehen Sie auf dem Bild, und wo stehen sie?
2 Was tragen sie?/Beschreiben Sie ihre Kleidung!
3 Wo kommen sie wohl her, und wo haben sie wohl übernachtet?
4 Was machen sie gerade?
5 Was werden sie wohl in den nächsten paar Stunden machen?

5

1 Wen sieht man durch die Tür?
2 Was hat er gerade gebracht?
3 Warum freut sich die Frau wohl?
4 Wen sieht man sonst auf dem Bild?
5 Wo ist er und was macht er?

4

1 Warum ist das junge Paar zu diesem Geschäft gekommen?
2 Beschreiben Sie den Verkäufer!
3 Beschreiben Sie den Wagen, den er ihnen zeigt!
4 Was kostet er?
5 Was hält der Mann vom Wagen? Und seine Frau?

6

1 Wessen Auto ist das wohl und wessen Motorrad?
2 Warum hat der Polizist gehalten?
3 Woher ist der Mann gerade gekommen, und was hat er gerade gemacht?
4 Was werden die beiden wohl jetzt machen?
5 Welche Läden sieht man auf dem Bild?

7 Im Schlafzimmer

8

1 Wo findet diese Szene statt?
2 Wieviele Autos sehen Sie auf dem Fußboden?
3 Wo liegen die Bücher?
4 Was macht der Junge?

(SEREB)

1 Wo sind die Kinder?
2 Was tragen sie?
3 Was macht der Vater?
4 Was wird die Familie wohl bald machen?

(WJEC)

9 Das Dorf

Answer, in German, *ten only* of the following questions about the picture – Das Dorf. (Your answers should be in *complete sentences*).

1 Was macht der Mann rechts?
2 Wie ist er hierher gekommen?
3 Was machen die Jungen?
4 Wo sitzt das Mädchen?
5 Wie kann man über den Fluß kommen?
6 Warum liegen die Kühe?
7 Welche anderen Tiere kann man sehen?

8 Was ist das größte Gebäude des Dorfes?
9 Was sieht man im Hintergrund?
10 Warum glauben Sie, daß es Sommer ist?
11 Wie sieht der Himmel aus?
12 Wohin fährt der Zug?

(WMEB)

Describing pictures: Points to remember

1 Keep statements about the pictures short and grammatically accurate.
Unless you are sure you can handle them, do not launch into long
sentences with complicated subordinate clauses. You can always express
such ideas more simply:
e.g. Obwohl es in Strömen regnet, gehen die jungen Leute aufs Land
spazieren.
More simply: Es regnet (in Strömen), aber die jungen Leute gehen
(trotzdem) spazieren. Sie gehen aufs Land.

2 Look for things you can say, rather than worry about things you can't!

3 Apart from saying what people in the pictures are actually doing, you can
also say what ......

— they have just done	... **hat/haben** | **gerade/(so)eben** ......
	ist/sind | + past participle
— they are in the process of doing	... **ist/sind gerade dabei,** ...... **zu** + inf.
— they are about to do	... **ist/sind im Begriff** ...... **zu** + inf.
— they might perhaps/probably do	... **wird/werden vielleicht/wohl/ wahrscheinlich** ...... + inf.
— they want/would like to do	... **will/wollen/möchte/möchten** ...... + inf.
— they intend to do	... **hat/haben vor,** ...... **zu** + inf.
— they are hoping to do	... **hofft/hoffen,** ...... **zu** + inf.
— they seem to be doing	... **scheint/scheinen,** ...... **zu** + inf.
— they are trying to do	... **versucht/versuchen,** ...... **zu** + inf.
— they have decided to do	... **hat/haben beschlossen,** ...... **zu** + inf.
— they are supposed to be doing	... **soll/sollen** ...... + inf.

Describing pictures: practice

Below are seven unconnected pictures. They do not make up a continuous
story. Treat each one as a separate scene, and describe each one of them
in at least ten sentences. Some ideas are suggested for the first two, but
you need not confine yourself to them. Here are some phrases which will
probably be a good starting point for describing any pictures in this sort
of exercise:

Die Szene | findet ...... (wo?) statt
          | passiert ...... (wo?)
Wir sind ...... (wo?)

Vorne/Im Vordergrund	ist/sind	...... (wer?)
Hinten/Im Hintergrund	sitzt/sitzen	...... (was?)
Links (vorne/im Hintergrund, *etc.*)	steht/stehen	
Rechts	liegt/liegen	
In der Mitte (des Bildes)	befindet sich/befinden sich	

Man sieht | einen Jungen, der ...... + *verb*
    | eine Frau, die ...... + *verb*
    | ein Kind, das ...... + *verb*
    | mehrere Kinder, die ...... + *verb*

Er/Sie/Es sieht | ...... (*adjective*) aus
Sie sehen |

Hinter	dem	ist/sind, *etc.* ...... (wer?)
Vor	der	...... (was?)
Neben, *etc.*	dem	
	den ...... (*pl.*)	
	ihm/ihr/ihm	
	ihnen	

Darauf	ist/sind, *etc.* ...... (wer?)	
Darin	...... (was?)	
Darunter, *etc.*		

1

Among other things you could say:

— Where the scene is taking place (i.e. in front of a school/in Germany).

— How many people you can see.

— Who the people are (i.e. English pupils/German families/teachers).

— Whether you think the coach has just arrived or is just leaving.

— Why the people in the background are walking towards the coach.

— What the teachers are doing and why (i.e. shaking hands/greeting one another?/taking leave of one another?).

— What the pupils in the coach look like (i.e. sad at leaving?/nervous at arrival?).

— What they will all do next (i.e. drive off?/get off coach?/drive off with families?).

2

- Where the scene is taking place (i.e. in a field/in the country).
- When it is taking place (i.e. in Winter/December/Xmas holidays?).
- What the weather is like (i.e. cold/has been snowing/freezing).
- What people are wearing (i.e. hats, gloves, warm clothing).

- What they are doing (i.e. making a snowman/skating/ sledging/playing in the snow).
- How many people you can see in the picture.
- Whose dog it might be.
- What the snowman looks like (i.e. big/has hat, pipe, etc.).

3

4

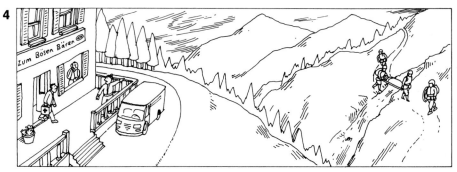

5

(WJEC)

6 Am Campingplatz

(NWREB)

7

(NWREB)

94

Writing compositions

Points to remember

1 Don't try to introduce impressive pre-learnt phrases which are irrelevant to the pictures, outline or theme set.

2 You are free to express the ideas involved in the story in any way you wish. Of course, certain vocabulary is essential to certain themes (i.e. accidents – **Krankenwagen**, **Krankenhaus**, **Arzt**, etc.), but there are usually several ways of expressing the general ideas.
e.g. If someone in the story rushes into a phone box, you could say he rushed (**stürzte**), hurried (**eilte**), ran (**lief/rannte**), went quickly (**ging schnell**); if someone comes back and finds his case missing, you could say it had disappeared (**war verschwunden**), wasn't there any more (**war nicht mehr da**), someone had stolen it (**jemand hatte ihn gestohlen**), someone had taken it (**jemand hatte ihn weggenommen**), etc.

3 Do not fall into the trap of working out sentences in English first, and then trying to translate them. Work the other way round: jot down any words and phrases (particularly verbs and an accompanying preposition, where appropriate – **gehen in** + accusative, **sitzen auf** + dative, etc.) and then use these to construct sentences. Use what you know; avoid what you're not sure about!

4 Think simple! Construct your composition in small units (i.e. subject + verb + direct object, subject + verb + preposition + noun, etc.). When you have done this, you may decide to join some of these small units together with conjunctions (**aber/als/weil**, etc.), but keep it simple initially.

5 Verbs are crucially important and the most common irregular verbs must be learnt thoroughly. Remember that, unlike in French, the imperfect tense can be used to express single actions in the past. If you find the perfect tense difficult, the imperfect is easier to manipulate, i.e. **er sah** rather than **er hat gesehen**, **er ging** rather than **er ist gegangen**. It avoids, of course, the problem of **haben** or **sein**.

6 You should, as far as possible, write equal amounts for each picture or section of the story. You will gain nothing by writing more than the number of words asked for. You can therefore work out roughly in advance how much you should be writing about each picture or section.

7 To help get your compositions off to a good start, and to round them off nicely, it is useful to draw up a list of phrases such as:
   a An einem (windigen) Aprilvormittag …; In den (letzten) Sommerferien …; Zu Weihnachten (letzten Jahres) …, *etc.*
   b Der Ausflug (*etc.*) war also eine Katastrophe!; Das war wirklich schade!; Ende gut, alles gut, wie man sagt! *etc.*

8 When you have finished, check your work carefully, but do so systematically! Don't just read it through hoping to detect the odd mistake; read it through several times, looking for specific things.
   e.g. Do the verbs all agree with the subjects? If using the perfect tense, have you used **sein** with verbs of motion? Is the word order in each sentence correct? Have you used the correct adjectival endings? etc.

Preliminary exercises

1 Imagine that the following pictures represent the first frames in a number of picture stories. In each case, say
   a where the person/people was/were sitting/standing, etc.
   b add what he/she/they was/were doing there
   c add when this was taking place

e.g.

a Die Familie Schmidt saß auf einem Feld.

b Die Familie Schmidt saß auf einem Feld und machte ein Picknick.

c An einem schönen Sommertag saß die Familie Schmidt auf einem Feld und machte ein Picknick.

im Büro sitzen / arbeiten

in der Küche sitzen / frühstücken

auf dem Bahnhof stehen / auf den Zug warten — Köln

im Garten stehen / plaudern

auf dem Sofa liegen / fernsehen

im Krankenhaus liegen / eine Zeitschrift lesen

die Landstraße entlang gehen / Brombeeren pflücken

durch die Stadt fahren / einen Parkplatz suchen

in der Stadt sein / Einkäufe machen

2 Practise saying what the weather was like on the day/morning/afternoon/evening in question by using the following verbs/expressions in the imperfect. Start each sentence with **An dem Tag/Vormittag/Nachmittag/Abend** …

e.g.

(in Strömen) regnen

An dem Tag, *etc.* **regnete** es (in Strömen).

schneien

(das Wetter) bitterkalt sein / frieren

windig sein

neb(e)lig sein

(das Wetter) heiß/ herrlich sein / (die Sonne) scheinen

gewittern / donnern und blitzen

3 Verbs with *haben* in the perfect

Give names to the characters in the following pictures, and practise saying what incident took place

a using the imperfect
b using the perfect (N.B. all these verbs take **haben**)
c adding an appropriate adverb from the following at the beginning of the sentences: **plötzlich/dann/(fünf Minuten**, *etc.*) **später/leider/zum Glück**; remembering, of course, the word order change.

e.g.

Ansichtskarten kaufen

a Erich **kaufte** Ansichtskarten.
b Erich **hat** Ansichtskarten **gekauft**.
c Dann | **kaufte** Erich Ansichtskarten.
| **hat** Erich Ansichtskarten **gekauft**.

duschen

(in der Hauptstraße) parken

einen Platz finden

den Bus (in die Stadt) nehmen

eine Panne haben

eine Burg besuchen

seine Schlüssel verlieren

den Zug verpassen

ihren Freund anrufen

die Kaffeekanne umstoßen

eine Dampferfahrt machen

sich verletzen/sich in den Finger schneiden

98

4 Verbs with *sein* in the perfect

Give names to the characters in the following pictures and practise saying what incident took place
a using the imperfect
b using the perfect (N.B. all these verbs take **sein**)
c adding an appropriate adverb from the following at the beginning of the sentences: **dann/kurz darauf/sofort/inzwischen/unglücklicherweise/ schließlich/endlich**; remembering, of course, the word order change.

e.g.

ins Kino gehen

a Sigrid **ging** ins Kino.
b Sigrid **ist** ins Kino **gegangen**.
c **Dann** | **ging** Sigrid ins Kino.
| **ist** Sigrid ins Kino **gegangen**.

in die Stadt fahren	zur Telefonzelle laufen/rennen	stolpern/hinfallen	auf einen Baum klettern
einschlafen	nach Deutschland fliegen	in Deutschland landen/ ankommen	in den Bus einsteigen
schwimmengehen	ins Schleudern geraten	dem Mann folgen	einer Freundin begegnen

1 Die Einladung

1 Wann hat der junge Mann seine Freundin angerufen? Wozu?

seine Freundin anrufen/mit seiner Freundin telefonieren
ins Kino einladen
die Einladung annehmen

2 Was hat das Mädchen gemacht, bevor der junge Mann angekommen ist?

sich die Haare waschen
sich schminken
sich umziehen

3 Woher hat sie gewußt, daß er angekommen war?

auf dem Sofa sitzen/auf ihn warten/eine Zeitschrift lesen
hupen/zum Fenster hinaussehen
ihren Freund sehen

4 Wie lange sind sie im Kino geblieben?

Schlange stehen (müssen)
einen spannenden Horrorfilm sehen

5 Was haben sie gegessen und getrunken?

ins Restaurant gehen
den Film besprechen

6 Um wieviel Uhr sind sie wohl zu Hause angekommen?

seine Freundin nach Hause fahren/bringen
sich verabschieden

2 Na, so was!

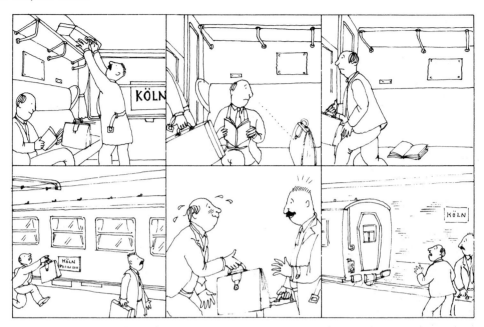

1 Wohin fuhr der eine Mann? Und der andere?

in Köln ankommen
sein Gepäck herunternehmen
sitzen bleiben/(weiter)lesen

2 Was hat der eine Mann beim Aufstehen nicht bemerkt?

das Abteil verlassen
seine Aktentasche dort lassen
es nicht bemerken

3 Wie hat der zweite Mann auf die Situation reagiert?

die Aktentasche schnell greifen
sein Buch auf den Sitz hinlegen
aus dem Abteil laufen

4 Wo war der erste Mann schon?

aus dem Zug aussteigen
dem ersten Mann nachlaufen
ihm zurufen

5 Was hat der Mann wohl gesagt, als er seine Aktentasche sah?

den ersten Mann einholen
die Aktentasche zurückgeben
erleichtert sein

6 Was hat der erste Mann wohl gesagt, als er sah, was passiert war?

sich umdrehen
sehen, daß .../wie ...
den Zug verpassen

3 Ausgerechnet das mußte passieren!

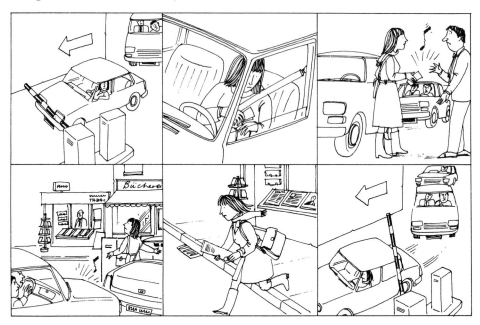

1 in die Stadt fahren
in einer Tiefgarage parken wollen
sich anstellen (müssen)
(endlich) an der Schranke
  ankommen
Kleingeld brauchen

2 ihre Handtasche aufmachen
im Handschuhfach suchen
kein Kleingeld finden
nur Scheine bei sich haben
(sehr) verlegen sein

3 aus dem Auto/Wagen aussteigen
einen Vorbeigehenden um
  Kleingeld bitten
leid tun
der Frau nicht helfen können

4 die Geduld verlieren/ungeduldig
  werden
hupen/anfangen zu hupen
einen Laden sehen/bemerken

5 schnell zum Laden laufen
in den Laden eilen
eine Zeitung kaufen
Kleingeld bekommen
zum Auto zurücklaufen

6 die Münzen einwerfen
seine Karte bekommen
(endlich) in die Tiefgarage fahren
  können
erleichtert sein

4 Die Rettung

1 am Strand ankommen
nicht weit vom Strand parken
die Badesachen usw.
auspacken/mitnehmen
an den Strand gehen

2 eine Decke auf den Sand/die
Erde legen
(sich) Liegestühle mieten
im Sand spielen/bauen
die Luftmatratze aufblasen

3 sich in einen Liegestuhl setzen/in
einem Liegestuhl sitzen
ins Wasser gehen
auf der Luftmatratze schwimmen

4 vor sich hintreiben/weit vom
Strand treiben

Hilferufe ausstoßen
vor Angst weinen
einen großen Schock bekommen
mit Entsetzen sehen, daß/wie …
(vergebens) versuchen ……
zu + inf.
den Jungen erreichen/zum
Jungen hinausschwimmen

5 den Jungen sehen
ihm ein Seil zuwerfen
ihn mit dem/am Seil ins Boot
hochziehen
ihn retten

6 ins Wasser gehen/zum Boot
hinauswaten
vom Boot hinunterklettern
ans Land tragen/bringen

5 Pilze sammeln

6 Der Tourist

7 Eine Unverschämtheit!

8

(WJEC)

9

(YHREB)

10

(AEB, 1981)

Free and guided composition

Constructing a story

Some kinds of composition question set out in quite detailed terms how the composition must develop. This, of course, leaves little room for imagination. Others, however, give short, vague, or open-ended instructions which allow you considerable freedom; in these cases, a little thought and planning will enable you to show off what you know and avoid what you aren't sure of! The following examples show how two such stories could be developed using only simple phrases:

a Write a composition entitled „Meine Sommerferien".

(ALSEB)

How long were the holidays this year? (sechs Wochen *etc.* Schulferien haben)
Did you stay at home? (nicht in die Ferien fahren; nicht verreisen; in ......
bleiben)
If you stayed at home, what did you find to do? (mit den Freundinnen/
Freunden spielen; nichts Besonderes machen/unternehmen; (meistens) zu
Hause bleiben/hocken; viel lesen/fernsehen; spazierengehen; radfahren;
Tennis *etc.* spielen)
Did you visit someone? Where? (Verwandte/Freunde in ...... besuchen)
Did you go on day trips? (Einen Ausflug/Ausflüge nach ...... (und ......)
machen)
To the seaside? (an die See/ans Meer fahren)
What did you do there? (baden; schwimmen; sich sonnen; ein Eis kaufen;
angeln; ein Boot mieten; eine Dampferfahrt machen)
Did you go away on holiday? (in die Ferien fahren; nach ...... verreisen)
How long did you stay? (14 Tage *etc.* in ...... verbringen; eine Woche *etc.*
in ...... bleiben)
How did you get there? (mit dem Zug/Auto/Schiff dorthin fahren; dorthin
fliegen)
What sort of accommodation? (zelten; im Hotel/Wohnwagen wohnen)
What was the weather like? ((die Sonne) scheinen;
kalt/windig/schön/gewittrig/ neblig sein)
What was the holiday like? (langweilig/prima/herrlich/eine Enttäuschung)
What did you bring back? (Andenken kaufen; ein Geschenk/Geschenke
für ...... kaufen)

b „Gestern sind Hans und Maria in die Stadt gefahren, um Einkäufe für
ihre Mutter zu machen."
Finish this story.

(SEREB)

Why did they go? (Mutter krank; Besuch haben/zu Besuch kommen)
What did they do before going? (eine Liste von Lebensmitteln von ihrer
Mutter bekommen/eine Liste von Lebensmitteln schreiben; ihre Mopeds
aus der Garage holen; zur Haltestelle gehen; (zehn Minuten *etc*.) auf den
Bus warten müssen)
How did they go? (mit dem Bus/auf ihren Mopeds fahren; am Marktplatz
aussteigen/ihre Mopeds auf dem Marktplatz *etc*. parken)
Did they do anything on the way into town? (unterwegs Benzin kaufen/
bekommen/besorgen; mit einem Nachbarn im Bus plaudern)
What did she need? (Obst/Zucker/Milch *etc*. brauchen;
Gemüse/Fleisch/eine Torte *etc*. kaufen müssen)
Where did they get these things? (...... in der Konditorei/beim
Gemüsehändler *etc*. kaufen/in den Supermarkt/zum Bäcker *etc*. gehen, um
...... zu kaufen)
Did they do anything in town besides shopping? (ins Plattengeschäft
gehen; sich Platten anhören/kaufen; ins Café gehen; eine Cola/einen
Kaffee trinken)
Did anything untoward happen? (das Geld/die Fahrkarten verlieren; den
Bus verpassen; eine Flasche Essig (auf den Boden) fallen lassen)
What were the consequences? (nicht wieder finden können/nicht
zurückbekommen; das Glas vom Bürgersteig *etc*. fegen; sehr spät nach
Hause zurückkommen; (Mutter) Angst haben)
Did they perhaps buy anything for her? (Blumen/Pralinen für ihre Mutter
kaufen; eine schöne Überraschung haben/sein)
What was mother's reaction? (den Kindern für ihre Hilfe danken/den
Kindern dankbar sein)

Guided compositions

a 1 Sie haben eine Wanderung gemacht. Wann? Mit wem? Was haben Sie
mitgenommen? Beschreiben Sie die Kleidung, die Sie getragen haben!
Was haben Sie unterwegs gesehen? Haben Sie sich unterwegs
aufgehalten? Warum?/Wozu? Um wieviel Uhr sind Sie wieder zu Hause
angekommen?

2 Sie sind zum Safaripark gefahren. Wann? Mit wem? Was hat der Eintritt
gekostet? Wieviele/Welche Tiere haben Sie dort gesehen? Durfte man die
Tiere füttern? Welche? Womit? Außer den Tieren, was gab es dort zu
sehen und zu tun? Haben Sie dort gegessen? Wie lange sind Sie dort
geblieben?

3 Sie hatten in letzter Zeit Geburtstag. An einem Wochentag? Am Wochenende? Wie haben Sie gefeiert? Haben Sie einen Besuch/Ausflug gemacht? Mit wem? Wohin? Oder haben Sie zu Hause Besuch gehabt? Was für Geschenke haben Sie bekommen? Haben Sie Geld bekommen? Wieviel? Was haben Sie damit gemacht?

4 Eines Abends haben Sie für Ihre Nachbarn Babysitting gemacht. Warum brauchten sie eine(n) Babysitter(in)? Wieviele Kinder hatten sie? Jungen oder Mädchen? Wie hießen sie? Wie alt waren sie? Wann sind Sie bei ihnen angekommen? Was haben Sie mit den Kindern gemacht, bevor sie ins Bett gingen? Und während sie im Bett waren? Welche Probleme/ Schwierigkeiten hatten Sie? Um wieviel Uhr sind die Eltern heimgekommen? Wo waren sie gewesen? Wieviel haben Sie für den Abend verdient?

5 Sie hatten eine(n) deutsche(n) Austauschpartner(in) bei Ihnen. Wann? Wie lange ist er/sie bei Ihnen geblieben? Schreiben Sie ein paar Einzelheiten über ihn/sie! Erzählen Sie was Sie mit ihm/ihr unternommen haben!

6 Write a composition of about 100–150 words, *in German* (in the Past Tenses), on the following subject, using some or all of the suggestions given:
A trip into the mountains
Osterferien – Schulgruppe – mit dem VW-Bus – wohin? – was für Kleidung? – Essen? – die Wanderung – wie lange? – Pause machen – die Rückkehr.

(WJEC)

7 Write a composition of about 100–150 words, *in German* (in the Past Tenses), on the following subject, using *some* of the suggestions given:
Imagine you flew to Düsseldorf last Summer to spend some time with your pen-friend. Describe briefly preparing for the journey, reaching the airport, what happened during the flight and your arrival in Düsseldorf.
aufstehen – um wieviel Uhr? – Haus verlassen – abfliegen – der Pilot – die Stewardess – Erfrischungen – Getränke – landen – begrüssen.

(WJEC)

8 Write in *German*, using past tenses whenever appropriate, *at least 180 words but not more than 200 words* on the following subject. State at the end the number of words used.

Tell the story outlined below, keeping to three paragraphs of about 60 words each. You may use as you wish the vocabulary suggested and may add any relevant detail.

You went to the station to meet your grandmother who was expected for a short stay with your family. But she wasn't on the train when it arrived. You returned home and told your parents what had happened. They were worried and wondered what had gone wrong.

Eventually the telephone rang and your grandmother explained what had happened and how she proposed to sort things out.

Großmutter abholen − Ankunft des Zuges − die vielen Reisenden − keine Großmutter. Wieder nach Hause − Eltern besorgt. Telefonanruf aus London − falschen Zug genommen − übernachten − wo? − ankommen − wann?

(WJEC)

b 1 You were in town one day. Why were you there? You saw an accident. Who was involved? What happened? Why did it happen? Who else saw it? How were you, or anyone else, able to help?

2 You went abroad with your family. Where? How did you get there? How long did you stay there? What was the weather like? How did this affect what you planned to do? What special food and drink did you have? What special things did you see and do?

3 You and some friends organized a Christmas school disco. What preparations did you make? It turned out to be a fiasco! What went wrong? What were the consequences?

4 You were camping. Where? With whom? There was a sudden change in the weather! How did this affect you? How did you manage to cope with the situation?

5 You wanted a certain sum of money last summer. What for? You managed to get a number of jobs to earn the money. How? Doing what? Describe the day when you could finally afford what you wanted!

6 Recently you got a new pet. What was it? Did you already have any? Did you fetch it or did someone bring it home? Was it bought or given to you? What was everyone's reaction? What did you give it to eat and drink? What did you do about accommodating/exercising it? Have you still got it?

7 Write a story using the following outline:
Out riding your bicycle in the country − a car parked by the roadside − doors wide open − occupants nowhere to be seen − mystery − end of story.

(YHREB)

8 Write a story using the following outline:
Arrive home − into living room − funny smell − direction of kitchen − open door − smoke pours in − send for fire brigade − cause of fire?

(YHREB)

9 Write in *German* a composition of 60–80 words about a night you went out with some friends. You may include some of the following ideas.

a The clothes you wore
b Who went with you
c Where you went

d How you got there
e Some of the things you did or saw
f The time you got home

(LREB)

Free compositions

a 1 Tell about a frightening experience you had recently.

2 Describe how you and your parents were able to help some fellow-travellers who had broken down in Germany last year.

3 Write about a day trip which you and your class went on to the seaside last summer.

4 Imagine that you have just seen a good film at the cinema. Tell a friend of yours what happened in the story.

5 Describe your arrival in a German town and how you found the way to your hotel (include conversation where appropriate).

(EMREB)

6 Write a composition using the title „Ein Umzug in ein anderes Haus".

(NWREB)

7 You went on a skiing holiday to Switzerland with a school party and as a project you had to write a diary in German. Write one full day's diary account.

(SEREB)

8 Write a composition in the Past Tenses on the following subject.
You have received DM40 (about £10) for your birthday. Describe how you spent it.

(WJEC)

9 Write about any personal experience you have had which made a Day to Remember.

(EAEB)

10 Beschreiben Sie einen Ihrer Lehrer (oder eine Ihrer Lehrerinnen) und sagen Sie, warum er/sie Ihnen gefällt (oder nicht gefällt)!

(SUJB)

111

11 Kurt and Karl find a handbag. They open it to try to discover the owner and then discuss what they shall do with it. Write the conversation which takes place between them during these events.

(ALSEB)

12 Letzte Woche fuhren Sie mit Ihrem Vater im Wagen. Plötzlich, mitten im Verkehr, blieb der Wagen stehen. Erzählen Sie, was passierte!

(NISEC)

13 While you were walking in the country near your home you were the only witness when a plane crash-landed. Describe what happened and how you helped.

(UCLES)

b Continue a story which begins with the words:

1 Die Schmidts wollten ihre englischen Freunde in London besuchen. Sie kamen kurz vor Mitternacht bei ihnen an. Im Haus brannte kein Licht ...

2 Ich zitterte vor Erregung, als ich das Papier vom Geschenk riß. Es war genau das, was ich mir gewünscht hatte ... ein Photoapparat!

3 „Hier ist Post für dich, Karin!" sagte Mutter. Karin machte den Brief auf. Sie konnte ihren Augen kaum trauen!

4 Frau Hebbel machte die Tür auf. Vor ihr stand ein Polizist!

5 Gegen fünf Uhr abends haben wir einen Campingplatz gefunden, der am Ufer eines großen Sees lag.

6 Continue the following story. Do not copy out this paragraph.
Hans hatte ein blaues Paket in der Hand, als er in die Apotheke ging. Erst zehn Minuten später, als er auf den Bus wartete, vermisste er das Paket. „Ich habe es wahrscheinlich in der Apotheke liegen lassen," dachte er und ging nach dem Geschäft zurück. Unterwegs sah er aber einen Mann, der ein blaues Paket in der Hand trug, über die Strasse gehen. Was tat Hans?

(EAEB)

7 Continue the following conversation:
Paul: Was hältst du von der Idee, Vater?
Vater: Das kann doch nicht dein Ernst sein!!

8 Continue the following conversation:
Manfred: Grüß Gott, Frau Schmidt.
Frau Schmidt: Grüß Gott, Manfred. Warum bist du heute nicht in der Schule?

Writing letters

Points to remember

1 When people write to real pen-friends they usually confine themselves to writing fact. Letters written for examinations, however, are a purely fictional exercise; you are free to answer your 'correspondent's' questions in any way you choose, inventing incidents, excuses, holidays, members of your family, pets, etc. as you think fit. Your main aim should be to make the letter interesting and display your knowledge of German.

2 Before you start the letter, think about which form of 'you' is appropriate for the type of letter you are writing. It is not a bad idea to jot down the one(s) you are to use, with the corresponding possessive adjective(s) at the top of the page as a reminder.

Du/Dich/Dir/Dein(e) will be used when writing or referring to:
— your correspondent
— a fictitious German brother/sister/parent/uncle/classmate, etc.

Ihr/Euch/Euer(e) will be used when writing or referring to:
— your correspondent and a member/members of his/her family (i.e. you two, you lot, all of you, etc.)
— fictitious German brothers/sisters/parents/classmates, etc.

Sie/Ihnen/Ihr(e) will be used when writing or referring to:
— one or both of your correspondent's parents
— a stranger/strangers (hotel owner(s)/camp site owner(s)/prospective employer(s), etc.

Du and **Ihr** can be mixed when **Du** refers to your correspondent and **Ihr** to the whole family:

e.g. „Wie geht es **Euch**?" (i.e. all of you) „Ich hoffe, es geht **Dir** jetzt besser ..." (i.e. your correspondent)

Note that in letters all pronouns meaning you/yours are written with a capital.

3 In addition to the actual letter, some Boards give extra instructions in English; make sure you deal with them in full. As well as answering direct questions in the letter, you should also comment wherever possible on statements made by the writer, and possibly asking further questions of your own. You can refer to a particular statement in the lead letter by:

a Changing the person of the verb and adding **also**, and then adding a short reaction.

e.g. *Lead letter:* „Ich bin im Examen durchgefallen ..."
Answer: „Du bist also im Examen durchgefallen. Das ist ja schade!"

b Using „Was ...... angeht/betrifft."

e.g. *Lead letter:* „Ich hoffe, Du hast einen interessanten Aufenthalt in Schottland gehabt ..."
Answer: „Was meinen Aufenthalt in Schottland angeht/betrifft, war ich ziemlich enttäuscht."

c Saying the writer is wrong in his/her assumption using **leider/unglücklicherweise**.

e.g. *Lead letter:* „Du wirst wohl bald in die Ferien fahren ..."
Answer: „Leider/Unglücklicherweise verreise ich dieses Jahr nicht."

d Saying the writer is right in his/her assumption using **tatsächlich/wie Du sagst**.

e.g. *Lead letter:* „Ich nehme an, die Nachricht war ein Schock ..."
Answer: „Tatsächlich/Wie Du sagst, war das ein großer Schock."

e Using one of the following:

Es freut mich	zu	hören,	daß ...... + *verb*
Es hat mich gefreut		lesen,	
Es hat mich betrübt		erfahren,	
Es tut mir leid			
tat			
Ich war erleichtert			
überrascht			
enttäuscht			

Die Nachricht über + *accusative* hat mich sehr erfreut
, daß ...... + *verb* wirklich erschüttert, *etc.*
Zu/Nur schade, daß ...... + *verb*
Es ist ein (wahres) Glück, daß ...... + *verb*

When your 'correspondent' has talked about his/her interests, hobbies, school subjects, etc., and you in turn want to tell him/her about yours, you can say:

Ich selbst/selber (habe, *etc.* ...)/Selbst habe ich ...
Ich persönlich (habe, *etc.* ...)/Persönlich habe ich ...
Ich, dagegen, (habe, *etc.* ...)
Ich (habe, *etc.*) leider ...
Auch ich (habe, *etc.* ...)

The following list of short phrases will be useful for reacting to pieces of news, real or imaginary:

Wie schön! Wie nett!
Da hast Du* aber Glück gehabt!
Ich beneide Dich (nicht) darum!
Das klingt schön/interessant/schrecklich!
Das muß schön/interessant/aufregend gewesen sein.
Wie nett von Dir!
Was für eine Enttäuschung! Wie ärgerlich!
Du mußt überrascht/erschrocken/enttäuscht gewesen sein!
Wie/Zu schade! Das ist (aber/doch recht) schade!
Es ist schade darum/um ihn, *etc.*
Da hast Du aber Pech gehabt! So ein Pech!
Das ist/war ja unerhört/schrecklich! Das ist aber schlimm!
Du mußt stolz darauf sein! Deine Eltern müssen stolz auf Dich sein!
Er/Sie hatte es (reichlich) verdient!
Ich gratuliere!
Ich freue mich | darauf!
              | auf (Deinen Besuch, *etc.*)!

Preliminary exercises

a Comment on the following letter excerpts, using any of the above phrases:
e.g. „Meine Mutter muß nächsten Monat ins Krankenhaus ...“
Deine Mutter muß also bald ins Krankenhaus. Das ist wirklich schlimm!

* The **Ihr** or **Sie** form should be used where appropriate.

or   Es tut mir leid zu hören, daß Deine Mutter bald ins Krankenhaus muß.

b Add any follow-up comments or questions which seem appropriate. Some suggestions are given in each case, but you need not restrict yourself to them.

1 „Ich habe DM800 in einem Preisausschreiben gewonnen ...“
(What sort of competition?/What did he/she have to do?/Has he/she spent the money yet?/What did he/she buy?/If not, what did he/she do with the money?)

2 „Meine Schwester wird als Au-Pair-Mädchen in Großbritannien arbeiten ...“
When is she coming to Great Britain?/Where will she be working?/How long will she be staying?/Will she have any free time?/At weekends, perhaps?/She could visit you/You and your parents would be pleased to see her)

3 „Ich habe mir gerade ein Moped gekauft ...“
(What sort/make?/How much did it cost?/Where did he/she get the money?/Did his/her parents pay?/Did he/she earn the money?/Where has he/she already been on it?)

4 „Ich habe gerade gehört, ich bleibe nächstes Jahr sitzen ...“
(Why?/Was he/she bad in all subjects?/In which subjects was he/she bad?/What was his/her parents' reaction?/Did they punish him/her?/Are any of his/her classmates staying down too?)

5 „Mein Vater ist seit letzter Woche arbeitslos ...“
(Where was he working?/Why did he lose his job?/Was he the only one?/Will he find another job easily?/Does his/her mother work?

6 „Mein amerikanischer Brieffreund hat mich nach den USA eingeladen ...“
(You have never been to the USA yourself/Has he/she been there already?/Is he/she going to accept the invitation?/When is he/she going?/Where exactly does the correspondent live?/How long will he/she be staying?/How will he/she be travelling?)

7 „Der Sohn meines Nachbarn wurde in einem Verkehrsunfall schwer verletzt ...“
(Was he in a car, on a motorbike, on foot, etc.?/Was anyone with him?/Where did the accident happen?/When?/How?/Is he in hospital?/How serious is it?)

8 „Wenn ich zu Euch komme, möchte ich London besuchen ...“

(Of course you'll be able to go there/It won't be possible because it's much too far/Suggest an alternative town/Say what it has to offer/Say your parents will be working, but you'll take him to London by train/What would he/she particularly like to see and do there?)

9 „Ich freue mich auf meinen Aufenthalt bei Euch ...“
(Your mother would like to know what he/she likes to eat/drink/What doesn't he/she like?/What is he/she interested in?/Where would he/she like to go during his/her stay?)

10 „Ich interessiere mich nicht für klassische Musik ...“
(You do; you can't stand pop music!/You don't either; you like pop music!/Does he/she like pop music?/Which British singers or groups does he/she know?/Who is his/her favourite singer/musician?/What is the most popular song/record in Germany at the moment?/How much do records/cassettes cost in Germany?)

11 „Wir ziehen in etwa drei Wochen um ...“
(Why?/Has his/her father got another job?/Where will they be living?/Is he/she glad/sorry?/Will he/she have to go to another school?)

12 „Nächste Woche ist Kirchweih ...“
(You don't know what 'Kirchweih' is/What happens?/Is it fun?/Where does it take place?/How long does it last?)

13 „Ich treibe viel Sport ...“
(You don't!/You do too!/What sports/games does he/she like best?/How often does he/she play?/Does he/she watch much sport on the television?/Has he/she ever won a cup/medal/championship?/Does he/she play in a school team?)

14 „Mein Bruder hat sich verlobt ...“
(Which brother?/Who is his fiancée?/What does she look like?/How old is she?/Is she nice?/Do you know her?/How did they celebrate their engagement?/Did they buy each other rings?/When are they getting married?)

15 „Mein Moped wurde gestern abend gestohlen ...“
(Where had he/she left it?/Has he/she got it back?/Has he/she informed the police?/Does this sort of thing happen often?/How much is it worth?/How is he/she going to get to school now?)

16 „Unsere Katze ist vorgestern verschwunden ...“
(The black and white cat you saw last year?/Not to worry – he'll come back/Cats often disappear for two or three days/Has it happened before?/His/Her brother/sister must be very upset/Have they still got the dog they had when you were there?/And the rabbits? etc.)

117

Beginning and ending letters

The following letter openings should be learnt:

Informal
Lieber Karl!*/Liebe Helga!
Lieber Vater!/Liebe Mutter!/Liebe Eltern!
Lieber Onkel Otto!/Liebe Oma!
Ihr Lieben!

More formal
Lieber Herr Braun!/Liebe Frau Mayer!/Liebes Fräulein Schmidt!
Lieber Herr und liebe Frau Müller!

Formal
Sehr | geehrter Herr Seipp!
      | geehrte Frau Schwarz!
      | geehrtes Fräulein Schnitzel!
Sehr geehrte Herren!
Sehr geehrter | Herr Doktor Grünbaum!
            | Oberstudienrat Appel!
Sehr geehrte Kollegin!

The following letter endings will be useful:

Informal
Viele/Herzliche Grüße
Bis bald/Schreib bald/Laß bald von Dir hören
Dein Sid/Deine Beryl
Dein englischer *etc.* Brieffreund/Deine englische *etc.* Brieffreundin

More formal
Mit freundlichen/herzlichen Grüßen

Formal
Hochachtungsvoll!

Note the following way of passing on other people's good wishes:
Mutter läßt (Dich) grüßen/Meine Eltern lassen (Euch) grüßen
and of getting your wishes passed on:
Laß | Deine Eltern | von mir/uns grüßen!
    | (den) Karl |
    | (die) Karin |
Grüße Deine Eltern bitte (von mir)

* Nowadays a comma may be used after letter openings, in which case the first paragraph begins with a small letter.

Note the special 'back-to-front' formula which applies to short messages of greeting found in Christmas cards, etc.

e.g.

Ein frohes Weihnachtsfest und ein glückliches Neues Jahr wünscht Dir *Deine Ingrid*	*Alles Gute zum Geburtstag wünschen Dir* *Petra und Otto*

Section A

Answer in German the following letters from 'correspondents' and various other fictitious German people. The first four letters are followed by hints about what you could say apart from answering any direct questions asked in the letters.

1

Gummersbach, den 18. Oktober

Lieber/Liebe ......!

Heute in der Schule habe ich Deinen Namen als Brieffreund(in) gekriegt. Ich hoffe, es macht Dir nichts aus, wenn ich meinen ersten Brief auf Deutsch schreibe. Wie Du siehst, heiße ich Heinz/Karin Metzger; meine Freunde nennen mich aber meistens „Metzi". Ich wohne mit meinen Eltern in Gummersbach und bin in der achten Klasse der Gerhardt-Grimm-Schule. Ich mag die Schule gern. Ich bin nicht besonders gut in Englisch; ich mag es aber, denn unsere Englischlehrerin ist sehr nett. Mein Lieblingsfach ist Sozi.

Ich bin 1.80 m groß; ziemlich groß also. Ich habe kurze blonde Haare und blaue Augen und trage eine Brille. Ich bin ziemlich sportlich; mein Lieblingssport ist Schwimmen. Von meinem Haus bis zum Schwimmbad ist es nur ein Katzensprung. Ich bin nicht musikalisch, das heißt, ich spiele kein Instrument. Ich habe aber eine große Sammlung von Platten. Und Du? Was machst Du in Deiner Freizeit?

Ich hoffe, Du kannst meine schlechte Handschrift entziffern. Ich mache jetzt Schluß, denn ich habe heute abend viele Hausaufgaben. Ich hoffe, bald von Dir zu hören.

Herzliche Grüße
Dein(e) Heinz/Karin

- Thank him/her for the letter. Say when you received it and that you are pleased to have a correspondent at last. Say how long you have been looking for one.
- You don't mind if he/she writes in German. You'll write all of your letters in German. Ask him/her to correct your mistakes.
- Tell him/her what your nickname is (if you have one).
- Is Gummersbach a village/a small town/a big town? Ask what it is like. Give a few details about the village/town you live in.
- He/She hasn't any brothers or sisters then. Give details of your family situation, the name of your school and some details about it. Ask how far he/she lives from his/her school.
- Which subjects are you good/bad at in school? What is your favourite subject? Have you a male or female German teacher? What is he/she like? Say you don't understand what 'Sozi' is and ask what it is.
- Are you a sportsperson too? If so, which sports do you like? Do you like swimming? What sporting facilities are there near your house? What is the pool he/she goes to like? What does it cost to go in?
- Are you musical? If so, what instruments do you play? What music do you like listening to? How many records/cassettes have you got? How much do LPs cost in Germany?
- Make a comment about his/her handwriting. What is yours like?
- Say you hope he/she will write again soon.

2   Grotthohl, den 28. Juni

Lieber/Liebe ...... !

Seit langem haben wir kein Lebenszeichen von Dir gehabt. Wie geht es Euch allen?

Wir nehmen an, Du kommst in den kommenden Ferien zu uns wie abgesprochen, und freuen uns schon auf Dich. Obwohl wir diesen Sommer nicht verreisen, d.h. wir werden die ganze Zeit bei uns in Grotthohl sein, sind meine Eltern etwas besorgt, weil sie noch nicht wissen, wann Du kommst, wie lange Du bleibst, und wo sie Dich abholen müssen. Wir nehmen an, Du fährst mit dem Schiff und der Bahn. Du weißt ja, Deinen Bruder laden wir gleichfalls ein, wenn er mitfahren will und darf. Wir müssen bald an die Vorbereitungen für Deinen Aufenthalt bei uns denken und würden auch gerne wissen, was Du in Deutschland unternehmen möchtest? Köln und Bonn sind natürlich einen Besuch wert; das Siebengebirge auch. Und eine Rheindampferfahrt muß jeder Tourist machen, oder?

Laß uns also wissen, was Dich interessiert und was Du gerne sehen

und besuchen möchtest, damit wir Dir einen möglichst schönen
Aufenthalt anbieten können.

　　Laß Deine Eltern von uns grüßen. Schreib möglichst bald wieder!
　　　　　　　　　　　　　Viele Grüße
　　　　　　　　　　　　　Dein(e) Jürgen/Margrit

— Apologize for not having written for so long. Explain why. Have you
　been away? Ill? Have you had no time to write? Too much school
　work? Other extra-curricular or social activities?
— Can you, in fact, go? If not, why not? Family problems? Alternative
　holiday arrangements? Money problems? If so, how do you intend to
　travel? By boat and train, as suggested? By plane, as this is quicker
　and less trouble (even if more expensive!)?
— Give the date and time of arrival at the station/airport. Or perhaps your
　parents are travelling to Germany and will be able to drop you off on
　the way. Ask whether they could spend a day/night at your
　correspondent's house.
— Can your brother come too? Isn't he very keen? Has he other
　arrangements? Would he like to go later? At Christmas, perhaps? At
　Easter? Next Summer?
— Is there anything you'd particularly like to do in Germany? What do
　you think about going to Cologne and Bonn? Ask what there is to see
　and do there (apart from visiting Cologne Cathedral, of course!)?
　Comment on the Siebengebirge? Do you know what it is? Do you like
　'mountains'? Have you climbed any before? How high are they? Do
　you get vertigo? Comment on the boat trip. Do you think you'll enjoy it?
— Mention a couple of things you are interested in and relate this to your
　visit (e.g. sport – can you go to a football match?/animals – have they
　any pets?/cycling – can you go for some bike rides? etc.)
— Say you are looking forward to meeting/seeing them. Ask him/her to
　suggest something you could bring as a present for his/her parents.

3　　　　　　　　　　　　　　　Hotel Propodos,

　　　　　　　　　　　　　　　　Dedalos, den 1. Juli

Hallo, Ihr Lieben!
　　Gestern sind wir auf der griechischen Insel Dedalos angekommen.
Das Wetter ist herrlich (vielleicht doch ein bißchen zu heiß!) und wir
waren heute den ganzen Tag am Strand. Im Moment sitze ich auf dem
Balkon unseres Hotels, nippe an einem Fruchtsaft und schreibe an
Euch. Ich kann kaum glauben, daß ich fast noch drei Wochen in
diesem Paradies vor mir habe! Ich habe gerade gegessen; das Essen ist
fantastisch! Man kann sowohl deutsche Gerichte als auch griechische

Spezialitäten bekommen.

Ich habe keine Ahnung, was Ihr für diesen Sommer vorhabt. Ich nehme an, Ihr verreist irgendwohin. Nach Cornwall, vielleicht, wie voriges Jahr?

Das Nachtleben scheint hier Spitze zu sein! Gestern abend waren wir nach der langen Hinreise sehr müde und sind ziemlich früh ins Bett gegangen; wir haben aber nicht schlafen können denn es spielte bis spät in die Nacht hinein laute Popmusik. Es muß überall auf der Insel Nachtklubs und Diskotheken geben. Es scheint hier abends viel los zu sein. Ich dusche mich gleich, ziehe mich um und gehe dann aus. Hoffentlich wartet ein Brief von Euch auf mich, wenn ich wieder zu Hause ankomme.

Alles Gute!
Herzliche Grüße
Peter/Sigrid

— Were you at home when the letter arrived? Did you find it when you got back from holidays?
— Did you know they were going to Greece? Say how lucky you think they are; you envy them.
— What is the weather like where you are? (What was it like when you were on holiday?) Where are you sitting writing your letter? How does this contrast with his/her situation?
— What did he/she do on the beach? Swim? Fish? Sail? Windsurf? Just laze about and sunbathe? Is he/she nice and brown?
— Do you know anything about Greek food? Have you ever eaten any? Ask for more details.
— Say where you went/are going on holiday this year. Cornwall, as suggested? For how long? Compare this with his/her three weeks. Who did you go/are you going with? Camping? Caravan? Hotel? How does this compare with Greece? What did you do/will you be doing? What was/is the nightlife like there? What else does the place have to offer?

4   München, den 21. November

Lieber/Liebe . . . . . . !

Die Schularbeiten haben in den letzten paar Tagen ein bißchen nachgelassen; ich habe daher jetzt Zeit, Dir das Neueste über uns zu erzählen. Heute sind wir alle gespannt auf Vaters Rückkehr von der Arbeit; er bekommt nämlich seinen neuen Wagen von der Firma. Wir wissen noch nicht, was er kriegt, das wird aber das allerneueste Modell sein. Mein Bruder hat sich letzte Woche ein Motorrad gekauft. Da er sein Moped nicht mehr brauchte, hat er es mir geschenkt!

Wir haben gerade im Fernsehen gesehen, daß es in der letzten Zeit bei Euch in England (/Wales/Schottland, *etc.*) viele Gewitter gegeben hat mit Überschwemmungen und großen Schäden an Häusern, usw. Hoffentlich war das nicht so schlimm, wie es sich anhört!

Am Wochenende muß ich auf eine Hochzeit. Das wird wohl sehr langweilig sein. Zum Glück kommt das sehr selten vor. Bald danach aber fahre ich mit meiner Klasse zum Wintersport. Ich werde den ganzen Tag auf der Piste verbringen! Wie war die Klassenfahrt, von der Du in Deinem letzten Brief schriebst? Wo seid ihr endlich hingefahren? Hat's geklappt? Habt Ihr viel Spaß gehabt?

Hast Du dieses Jahr einen Ferienjob für die Weihnachtsferien gefunden? Bei uns sind Ferienjobs sehr dünn gesät.

Was sind Euere Weihnachtspläne? Bald müssen wir an Euer Weihnachtspäckchen denken. Wir werden was Schönes für Euch aussuchen!

Bis bald!

Euer(e) Rainer/Renate

— If you are writing before Christmas ... Tell them not to spend too much on presents for you. Wish them a Happy Christmas and a Happy New Year. Say you have sent/will soon be sending their Christmas parcel off. Say what you intend to do for Christmas. Stay at home? Go to relatives? To friends? Have you found a job? Doing what? Where? For how long? Was it easy to find? How much will you be earning?

— If you are writing after Christmas ... Thank them for the cards and presents they sent. Comment on what individual members of the family thought of their presents. Say you hope your parcel to them arrived safely, and that you hope they liked their presents. Say what other presents you had. Say where you spent Christmas and give a few details about how it went. Did you get a holiday job? Doing what? Where? For how long? How much did you earn? Was it difficult to find?

— How was school work towards the end of the Autumn Term?

— Ask what sort of car they got. Have you still got the same car?

— Make a comment about his luck in getting the moped. Have you got one? Are you hoping to get a motorbike/car later? How old must you be to ride a moped and motorbike/drive a car in Germany? How much do mopeds cost in Germany? Tell him/her what they cost over here.

— What has the weather been like recently? How bad were the 'storms'? Were you affected? Say that reports are often exaggerated on the television!

— Ask who got married. Someone in the family? A friend? Do you know him/her? Was the wedding really that bad?

— What do you think of him/her going skiing? Can you ski? How well?
How many times have you been? Where did you learn? Say he/she is
lucky to live near mountains. (Or perhaps you don't understand the
expression 'auf der Piste' – Ask what it means)
— Where did your class go? Was it a good day? Any mishaps? Money
lost? Pupils lost? Coach broke down? Rained all day, etc.

5 Imagine that you are Sabine's friend; reply to the following letter:

London, den 15. August

Lieber/Liebe ......!

Viele herzliche Grüße aus England. Ich besuche gerade meine
Brieffreundin Mary in London. Ihre Eltern haben ein Haus am
Stadtrand, aber wir fahren fast jeden Tag in die Stadt. Es ist einfach
toll, alles, was wir von den Photos in unserem Englischbuch kennen,
in Wirklichkeit zu sehen!

Marys Brüder und Schwestern sind auch ganz nett, aber wir
machen nicht sehr viel zusammen, weil sie fast jeden Abend in die
gleiche Disko gehen. Das finde ich zu langweilig.

Mit meinem Englisch klappt es jetzt ganz gut, aber am Anfang
habe ich fast nichts verstanden. In Deutschland hast Du wohl keine
Gelegenheit gehabt, Englisch zu sprechen, oder?

Und wie geht's Dir? Hoffentlich bist Du wieder ganz gesund. So
was Dummes, daß Du Dir das Bein kurz vor den Ferien brechen
mußtest! Kannst Du schon wieder laufen?

Ich vermisse Dich und die Clique sehr und habe ein bißchen
Heimweh. Drei Wochen sind eine lange Zeit – ein Brief von Dir
würde mich ja aufmuntern! Habt Ihr gemeinsam etwas Interessantes
unternommen? Wer in der Clique ist verreist?

Ich werde nächste Woche einen Einkaufsbummel machen, um alle
Geschenke und Andenken auf einmal zu kaufen. Dir möchte ich auch
etwas mitbringen kaufen. Laß mich mal wissen, was Dir besonders
gefallen würde. Der letzte englische Hit, vielleicht? Englischer
Lesestoff?

Ich freue mich darauf, von Dir zu hören.

Viele Grüße,
Deine Sabine

6   Hagersdorf, den 3. Mai

Sehr geehrter Herr/Sehr geehrtes Fräulein ......!

Es wird Sie wohl überraschen, einen Brief von einem
„Unbekannten" zu erhalten, besonders wenn es sich um einen
Deutschen handelt! Ein Unbekannter bin ich eigentlich nicht ganz,
denn wir haben uns flüchtig unterhalten, während Sie voriges Jahr bei
den Müllers in Hagendorf waren. Ich bin nämlich ein Nachbar der
Müllers, Besitzer der Fabrik, die gleich hinter dem Haus der Familie
Müller steht. Vielleicht erinnern Sie sich an mich.

Im Laufe unseres kurzen Gesprächs haben Sie gesagt, Sie hätten
gern einen Ferienjob in Deutschland. Wenn das tatsächlich Ihr Ernst
war, und falls Sie diesen Wunsch noch haben, kann ich Ihnen so eine
Stellung bei uns in der Firma anbieten.

Unterkunft wäre kein Problem, denn die Müllers sind bereit, Sie
unterzubringen, oder Sie könnten auch bei uns wohnen. Sie würden
natürlich ein eigenes Zimmer haben. Joachim, mein Sohn, der etwa in
Ihrem Alter ist, freut sich schon darauf, daß Sie zu uns kommen, denn
er möchte sein Englisch verbessern.

Wenn Sie an dieser Idee interessiert sind, bitte ich Sie
(postwendend, wenn überhaupt möglich) zu antworten. Wir werden
dann Näheres über die Stellung besprechen.

In der Hoffnung, bald von Ihnen zu hören, verbleibe ich mit
freundlichen Grüßen,

                                          Ihr Otto Krause

7   Düsseldorf, den 3. Februar

Lieber/Liebe ......!

Dies ist ein SOS-Ruf! Kannst Du mir helfen?

Meine Klasse muß eine Arbeit über einen typischen Schultag in
verschiedenen Ländern der Welt schreiben. Jeder von uns hat ein Land
zugeteilt bekommen, und ich habe Großbritannien gekriegt! Zum
Glück! Stell Dir bloß mal vor, ich hätte China, oder sogar Tibet
kriegen können!

Ich hatte ein paar Einzelheiten in einem alten Lehrbuch gefunden,
dann habe ich an Dich gedacht! Würdest Du mir einen typischen
Schultag beschreiben d.h. wann die Schule beginnt, wie lange die
Unterrichtsstunden dauern, usw.? Es würde mir auch sehr helfen,
wenn Du mir eine Kopie von Deinem Stundenplan schicken würdest.
Ich habe auch gehört, Ihr habt jeden Vormittag ein „assembly" –
darüber muß ich also auch ein paar Zeilen schreiben. Was ist das

                                                              125

eigentlich? Was für Klubs und Vereine hat man gewöhnlich in englischen Schulen? Welche Sportarten treibt man in den meisten Schulen? Wann finden Spiele gegen andere Schulen statt? Vergiß nicht zu sagen, wieviele Hausaufgaben Ihr bekommt! Da der Titel „Ein typischer Schultag in Großbritannien" lautet, muß ich auch etwas über Schottland, Wales und Nordirland schreiben. Weißt Du vielleicht, ob die Schule dort anders ist als in England?

Hauptsache, Du schreibst sofort, denn die Arbeit muß in 14 Tagen fertig sein!

Viele Grüße,
Dein(e) Henning/Christine

8   Bayreuth, den 8. Mai

Lieber/Liebe ......!

Ich hatte geplant, heute mit ein paar Schulkameradinnen und -kameraden ins Grüne zu radeln. Es regnet aber in Strömen, und das mußte leider ausfallen. Ich muß sagen, ich bleib nicht gern zu Hause, sogar wenn es regnet! Lesen, vor dem Fernseher hocken ... das kann ich einfach nicht leiden. Ich bekam gerade einen Anruf mit dem Vorschlag, wir sollten wegen des schlechten Wetters ins Kino gehen, um einen doofen Thriller zu sehen. Ich gehe hin, weil die anderen das wollen, aber so was interessiert mich nicht.

Das ist aber eine gute Gelegenheit, mich an meinen Schreibtisch zu setzen, und an Dich zu schreiben.

Wir hatten gerade eine schöne Nachricht von meinem älteren Bruder – seine Frau hat ihr Baby bekommen! Kein Wort aber von meiner Schwester, die vor ein paar Wochen mit ihrem Mann nach den USA umzog! Ich hoffe, es geht ihr gut, und sie lebt sich dort gut ein.

Hast Du die Resultate Deiner Prüfungen bekommen? Hoffentlich hat's gut geklappt! Ich weiß, Du machtest Dir große Sorgen darüber. Wie geht es Deinen Eltern? Gefällt Deinem Vater sein neuer Job? Sechzig Meilen sind ein langer Weg zur Arbeit. Wie kommt er damit zurecht? Du siehst ihn wohl abends viel weniger, oder? Während ich diesen Brief schrieb, hat sich das Wetter ein bißchen aufgeklärt. Der Regen hat jetzt aufgehört. Vielleicht ist unsere Radfahrt doch noch nicht ins Wasser gefallen!!

Bis bald!
Dein(e) Karl/Margit

126

9 The secretary of your local Judo Club has received the following letter from a similar club in Germany. Answer it on his behalf:

a accepting the offer and giving the details asked for.

b declining the offer and giving reasons.

c agreeing to a meeting in principle, but putting forward different proposals.

Bochum, den 30. Januar

Sehr geehrter Herr Schriftführer!

Der Judoverein Bochum hat mich beauftragt, an Sie zu schreiben, um mich nach der Möglichkeiten eines Wettkampfes zwischen unseren beiden Vereinen zu erkundigen. Wenn es möglich wäre, solch einen Wettkampf zu organisieren, schlagen wir vor, daß wir zuerst zu Ihnen kommen, und zwar in den kommenden Osterferien. Ich hoffe, eine eventuelle Gruppe selbst nach England begleiten zu können.

Wir würden gerne ein ganzes Wochenende bei Ihnen bleiben, damit wir die Gelegenheit wahrnehmen könnten, London zu besuchen. Wir würden deswegen an einem Freitagabend eintreffen und am Sonntagabend wieder abfahren, und zwar mit dem Flugzeug Köln–Heathrow. Genauere Termine könnten natürlich später besprochen werden.

Das Rückspiel könnte dann im Sommer bei uns in Deutschland stattfinden. Ich bitte Sie daher, mir folgendes mitzuteilen:

Ist das Unternehmen überhaupt möglich? Was die Unterkunft angeht, wären Ihre Vorschläge sehr willkommen. Vielleicht könnten die Mitglieder der beiden Gruppen sich gegenseitig unterbringen? Wären Sie bereit, einen Ausflug nach London für uns zu organisieren, oder organisieren zu lassen? Das würden wir selbstverständlich alles bezahlen.

In der Hoffnung, uns einmal persönlich kennenzulernen, verbleibe ich mit freundlichen Grüßen,

Ihr Deutscher Kollege
Hans Barsch

10 Below is a letter which you have received from a pen-friend in Germany. Write a reply in 120–150 words in German, remembering to set out your letter as a German would. You should try to deal with all the points in the pen-friend's letter.

Mainz, den 12. April 1982

Lieber/Liebe ......!

Es freut mich sehr, daß Du im August drei Wochen bei uns verbringen wirst. Bist Du schon einmal in Deutschland gewesen? Auf jeden Fall mußt Du mir sagen, was Du am liebsten in der Freizeit machst. Ich spiele gern Tennis; was für Sportarten treibst Du am liebsten? Hast Du andere Hobbys?

In Deinem letzten Brief hast Du geschrieben, daß Du am 3. August in Mainz ankommst. Wie fährst Du hierher? Und wo sollen Vati und Mutti Dich abholen?

Es fällt mir ein, daß ich kein Foto von Dir habe. Du mußt mir schreiben, wie Du eigentlich aussiehst, damit wir Dich leicht finden können.

Mutti möchte wissen, was Du am liebsten ißt. Normalerweise ißt meine Familie um halb zwei und dann abends um sieben.

Hast Du Tiere gern? Wir haben einen netten Hund, der Fritz heißt. Was für Haustiere hast Du?

Bitte schreib mir, was Du noch über meine Familie und meinen Wohnort wissen möchtest.

Mit besten Grüßen,
Dein/Deine Karl/Mitzi   (EAEB)

11 Read the following letter carefully. Write a suitable reply in German. Your letter should be from 100 to 130 words in length. Conventional introductory and concluding phrases forming part of the composition should not be reckoned in the total number of words. You may choose to reply in your own name. Replies may be addressed to a male or female correspondent.

Hannover, den 2. Mai 1983

Lieber Kenneth!

Vielen Dank für Deinen letzten Brief. Ich freue mich sehr auf meinen ersten Besuch in Schottland.

Du hast mir gesagt, daß wir mit Deinen Freunden auf dem Lande zelten könnten. Das wäre toll!

Schreib, bitte, und teile mir Deine Pläne für den Ausflug mit. Was für Vorbereitungen müssen wir machen? Wie und wohin werden wir fahren? Wie lange werden wir dort bleiben? Wie werden das Wetter und die Landschaft sein? Was soll ich mitbringen zum Anziehen? Was gibt es dort zu tun?

Und Deine Freunde und Freundinnen? Werde ich mit ihnen gut auskommen?

Laß bald von Dir hören. Ich möchte so viel wissen und bin schon so aufgeregt.

Mit herzlichen Grüßen,
Dein Uwe   (SEB)

Section B

Write letters from the following instructions:

1 Write a letter to a German pen-friend thanking him/her for the card and present he/she sent for your recent birthday. Say when they arrived. Say what you thought of the present. Tell him/her about the other presents you got and who bought them for you; tell him/her how much money you got and what you intend to buy or do with it. Say how you spent your birthday.

2 Write to a 'Fremdenverkehrsverein' in Northern Bavaria (Nordbayern) explaining that you and your family intend camping there in the following summer. Give the dates of your proposed holiday. Ask for a list of campsites and information about prices. Ask for a map of the area and plans of the major towns. Enquire about places of interest in the area and any special events which will be taking place during your stay.

3 Imagine that you have a friend who would like to go to Germany (or Austria or Switzerland) but hasn't any friends there. Write to a family you know there and ask if they can help in any way. Tell them about your friend; you could include details such as age, appearance, character, hobbies and interests, parents, home, when he/she would like to go there, and whether he/she would prefer to exchange or be a paying guest.

4 You have just given a party at your home to which you invited a large number of friends. Unfortunately lots of things went wrong, problems arose and there was a lot of silly, irresponsible behaviour. Your parents were not amused. Relate what happened and your parents' reactions in a letter to a German pen-friend.

5 You have seen an advert in an English paper for a house-swap with a German family. Write to them (invent a name!) giving details of the accommodation you can provide. Suggest a length of stay and dates which would suit you. Give some details about the town/area you live in and suggest some things they could do during their stay.

6 Write a letter to your German pen-friend telling him/her about the youth club you go to. Tell him/her how many people go to it, what facilities there are. Talk about special events and excursions there have been, or that will be taking place in the future. Say on which evening(s) and at what time the club is open, and how much it costs to go/join. Say what you particularly like doing there. Offer to take him/her there when he/she comes over to Great Britain.

7 Write to a German pen-friend and, after the usual pleasantries, tell him/her about something exciting (or amusing, or frightening) which happened to you last weekend.

8 You have recently been on an exchange visit to France. Write to your German pen-friend telling him/her about the journey, your impressions of your exchange partner, his/her family, the food, and your partner's school.

9 Imagine that you have been having some very abnormal weather conditions in the part of the country where you live (drought? storms? blizzards?). Write to a German pen-friend, telling him/her about it, how long it has been happening, and how it has been, and is, affecting you and your family, friends, and neighbours.

10 You stayed in a hotel in Germany last Summer and had a good holiday there. Write to the proprietor to book again for this year, stating precisely the accommodation you require for you and your family/friends and also mentioning what you particularly enjoyed about your previous stay there.

(**YHREB**)

11 A German helped your father repair his car when it broke down on holiday in Germany last year. On behalf of your parents, write him a letter, thanking him and inviting his family to stay with you, when they visit England this year. Give directions to your house, and tell them what you plan to do during their stay.

(**WMEB**)

12 Whilst on the aircraft on the return flight after a holiday in Germany your mother discovers that she has left her bag with all her money in the airport restaurant.

Write a letter in German to the airport manager on behalf of your mother, describing what has happened, what the bag looks like and what was in it. Ask the manager to send the bag, if it has been found, to the German friends with whom you were staying and explain that your father expects to fly back to Germany on business soon and will be able to collect the bag then.

Pay attention to the correct form of address and to the correct beginning and ending for such a letter.

(**WJEC**)

13 Imagine that you are either the boy or the girl in the series of pictures opposite. The incidents in the pictures took place two weeks ago near your home in England. Write a letter of between 120–150 words in German to a German-speaking pen-friend describing what happened. Remember to lay out your letter as a German person would. Use past tense, except where other tenses may be more appropriate, e.g., in conversation.

1

2 to collide = zusammen | prallen
hurt = verletzt

3

4 bandage = der Verband

(derived from an EAEB examination)

Grammar survey

Nouns

Articles

All nouns are divided into three groups or genders: masculine (m), feminine (f), and neuter (n). Corresponding to these are the indefinite articles:

m	f	n
ein	eine	ein

and the definite articles:

m	f	n
der	die	das

It is wise to learn each noun with its **der**, **die**, **das** label.

Plural of nouns

The plural of **der**, **die**, **das** is in each case **die**. Unfortunately one cannot make a noun plural by adding an **-s**, as one can for most English nouns. There are various plural forms in German. In dictionaries a dash is usually used to represent the singular noun, and changes, if any, are indicated thus:
der Wagen (**-**) i.e. plural **die Wagen**
der Bruder (**˙˙**) i.e. plural **die Brüder**
die Schwester (**-n**) i.e. plural **die Schwestern**
The plural form should be learnt whenever a new noun is met.

Cases*

Nominative
The **der**, **die**, **das** labels which one learns with nouns and their **ein**, **eine**, **ein** equivalents, are all in the *nominative* case. So too is the plural form **die**. This case is used to indicate the subject of the verb:
e.g. **Der** Lehrer kommt
Ein Junge hat die Grippe
Die Kinder spielen

Accusative
When a noun is the *direct object* of the verb, the masculine singular of its indefinite article (**ein**) and its definite article (**der**) become **einen** and **den** respectively:
e.g. Hier ist der Lehrer, *but*: Ich sehe **den** Lehrer
Ein Bruder ist krank, *but*: Ich habe **einen** Bruder
The accusative case is also required after certain prepositions (see p. 145).

Genitive
The *genitive* expresses ownership and corresponds to the English *'s*. The genitive is also required after certain prepositions (see p. 146). To form the genitive of proper nouns it is usually only necessary to add an **s** (no apostrophe):
e.g. Karl**s** Buch
Die Hauptstadt Frankreich**s**
Die Straßen London**s**

In the singular, **der**, **die**, **das**, **ein**, **eine**, **ein** change to:

m	des ......(e)s,	eines ......(e)s
f	der ......,	einer ......
n	des ......(e)s,	eines ......(e)s

Note that **-s** or **-es** (depending on

---

* A table setting out the full case system, along with corresponding adjectival endings, is given on pp. 150–1.

ease of pronunciation) is added to the end of masculine* and neuter nouns:

e.g. das Auto **des** Lehrer**s**
das Dach **des** Haus**es**
but das Heft ein**er** Schülerin

In the plural **die** changes to **der**.

e.g. die Eltern **der** Kinder

Dative

The *dative* case is used to indicate the *indirect object*, i.e. the person to whom something is given, offered, promised, handed, etc. The dative is also required after certain prepositions (see p. 145). The dative form of the indefinite and definite articles is, respectively:

m	f	n
einem	einer	einem
dem	der	dem

In the plural, **die** changes to **den**, and **-n** or **-en** is added to the plural form of the noun, unless it already ends in **-n**:

e.g. die Mädchen → **den** Mädchen
die Gärten → **den** Gärten
but die Häuser → **den** Häuser**n**
die Leute → **den** Leut**en**

An exception to the above is the group of nouns of foreign origin, the plural of which is **-s**. These do not require **-s** or **-es** to be added:

e.g. die Büros → **den** Büros
die Hotels → **den** Hotels

There are a few other foreign plurals which do not require **-n** or **-en** in the dative plural, but they are not likely to be needed, except perhaps **das Examen** (pl. **Examina**). Note that

---

* A group of masculine nouns is an exception to this. See Weak Masculine Nouns, below.

kein, the possessive adjectives, **dieser, jener, jeder, solcher** and **welcher** all undergo the same changes as **ein, eine, ein, der, die, das** in the various cases. (See tables on pp. 150–1.)

Weak masculine nouns

One group of masculine nouns (the plural of which is always **-n** or **-en**) is known as 'weak' masculine. The pattern of such nouns is given in the tables on pp. 150–1 and nouns which follow this pattern are indicated in the end vocabulary.

Verbs

In vocabularies and dictionaries verbs are listed in their *infinitive* form, e.g. **spielen**, to play. The different persons (e.g. I, you) and tenses (e.g. present, imperfect) are shown by different endings.

Persons of the verb

The persons of the verb are **ich** (I), **du** (you – *familiar*), **er** (he), **sie** (she), **es** (it), **man** (one), **wir** (we), **ihr** (you – *familiar plural*), **Sie** (you – *formal singular and plural*), **sie** (they). Note that **er** and **sie**, as well as meaning 'he' and 'she', can also both mean 'it' when referring to an inanimate object which is masculine or feminine:

e.g. **Der Tisch** ist alt – **Er** ist alt.
Die Tasche ist grün – **Sie** ist grün.

Du, Sie and **Ihr** all mean **you** but are used in different situations. **Du** is the familiar form and is used to address a friend, a member of the family (including a pet!), and when a grown-up speaks to a youngster. Young people use it to speak to one another even when they are meeting for the first time.

Ihr is the plural of **du** and is used to address two or more of the above.
Sie is formal and is used to address one or more strangers, among grown-ups in a formal situation, and when youngsters speak to grown-ups other than close family.

Present tense

In English there are three ways of expressing the present tense:
I play (every day, often, etc.)
I am playing (now, this morning, etc.)
I do play/do you play?

In German there is only one equivalent for these three forms:
ich spiele

Regular verbs have the following pattern:

ich spiel**e**	wir spiel**en**
du spiel**st**	ihr spiel**t**
er/sie/es/man spiel**t**	Sie spiel**en**
	sie spiel**en**

When an infinitive ends in **-ten** or **-den**, an extra **e** is added to the second and third person singular endings to make it easier to say:
e.g. arbei**ten** → du arbeit**est**
er arbeit**et**
re**den** → du red**est**, er red**et**

Note also: reg**nen** → es regn**et**.
Some verbs change or modify the root vowel in the **du** and **er/sie/es/man** forms:
a becomes **ä**, e.g. h**a**lten
→ du h**ä**ltst, er h**ä**lt
au becomes **äu**, e.g. l**au**fen
→ du l**äu**fst, er l**äu**ft

e becomes **ie**, e.g. s**e**hen
→ du s**ie**hst, er s**ie**ht
or **i**, e.g. n**e**hmen
→ du n**i**mmst, er n**i**mmt

The most common of these verbs are given in the verb list on pp. 152–4. Certain common verbs are irregular and must be learnt individually. These are also given in the verb list.

Questions

Questions are formed in German by inverting the subject and verb, as in English:

Er ist ...... → **Ist er** ......?
Karl kommt. → **Kommt Karl**?

Modal verbs

One group of irregular verbs is known as *modal auxiliary verbs*. The singular forms are irregular and must be learnt; the plural forms are regular.

können	**wollen**
(*to be able, can*)	(*to want*)
ich **kann**	ich **will**
du **kannst**	du **willst**
er **kann**	er **will**
wir **können,** *etc.*	wir **wollen**, *etc.*

müssen	**sollen**
(*to have to, must*)	(*to be supposed to, to be to*)
ich **muß**	ich **soll**
du **mußt**	du **sollst**
er **muß**	er **soll**
wir **müssen,** *etc.*	wir **sollen**, *etc.*

mögen	**dürfen**
(*to like*)	(*to be allowed to*)
ich **mag**	ich **darf**
du **magst**	du **darfst**
er **mag**	er **darf**
wir **mögen**, *etc.*	wir **dürfen**, *etc.*

Modal verbs are usually used in conjunction with an infinitive which stands at the end of the sentence:
Ich kann die Musik nicht gut **hören.**
Ich muß jetzt nach Hause **gehen.**

Imperative

There is an order form to correspond to each of the **du**, **wir**, **ihr** and **Sie** forms of the verb. The **wir**-form imperative has the meaning 'let's ...!' Regular verbs form their imperatives thus:
du machst → **mach**! (i.e. drop **du** and **-st** ending)
wir machen → **machen wir**! (i.e. invert subject and verb)
ihr macht → **macht**! (i.e. drop ihr)
Sie machen → **machen Sie**! (i.e. invert subject and verb)

The **du**-form of most irregular verbs is formed in the same way as that of regular ones:
du sprichst → **sprich**!
du nimmst → **nimm**!

Those verbs which take an Umlaut in the second and third person singular drop this in the imperative:
du f**ä**hrst → f**a**hr!
du l**äu**fst → l**au**f!

Mal is often added to imperatives as an extra 'urging word':
Komm **mal**!
Gehen wir **mal** ins Kino!

The verb **sein** is irregular and must be learnt carefully:
sei! seien wir! seid! seien Sie!

Separable and inseparable verbs

Some verbs have an infinitive which is made up of a simple verb and a stressed prefix, all written as one word, e.g. **mitkommen, heimgehen.**

These are known as separable verbs. In the present tense and the imperative the prefix breaks off and goes to the end of the sentence:
e.g. Ich **gehe** jetzt **heim**.
Komm mal **mit**!

After modal verbs the parts remain together:
e.g. Ich will jetzt **heimgehen**.
Ich kann nicht **mitkommen**.
There are more details about separable verbs on p. 138 under the heading 'perfect tense' and on p. 139 in notes on the use of **zu**.

Some verbs have an infinitive which is made up of a simple verb and an unstressed prefix. These prefixes are inseparable. The most common are **ver-** and **be-**. Others are **emp-**, **ent-**, **er-**, **miß-**, and **zer-**.
e.g. besuchen, behalten, versuchen, verstehen, verkaufen

In the present tense and imperative inseparable verbs behave like simple verbs:
e.g. Ich besuche meine Großeltern.
Behalten Sie es!
Verstehst du das?

There are more details about inseparable verbs on p. 138 under the heading 'perfect tense'.

Reflexive verbs

These verbs can be recognized in the infinitive by their reflexive pronoun **sich**, e.g. **sich verletzen**. The usual meaning of the reflexive pronoun is *oneself*: **sich** verletzen − to hurt oneself.

The pronouns must, of course, change according to the person of the verb (myself, yourself, etc.). Here is a typical present tense showing all of the pronouns:

ich verletze **mich**	wir verletzen **uns**
du verletzst **dich**	ihr verletzt **euch**
er | verletzt **sich**	Sie verletzen **sich**
sie |	sie verletzen **sich**
es |	
man |	

In many cases a reflexive pronoun is required in German where it is not required in English:

e.g. **sich waschen** to wash (i.e. oneself)
sich (hin)setzen to sit down (*literally*: to set oneself down)
sich konzentrieren to concentrate (*literally*: to concentrate oneself)

The pronoun **sich** can also mean *one another*:

e.g. **sich wiedersehen** to see one another again
sich treffen to meet one another

When there is a direct object other than the pronoun, the latter is put into the *dative* and shows *to whom*, *for whom*, or *for whose benefit* the action is done:

e.g. Ich kaufe **mir** ein neues Hemd.
Ich wasche **mir** die Hände.

Note that **sich** is both accusative and dative:

e.g. Er wäscht **sich** (*accusative*).
Er wäscht **sich** die Hände (*dative*).

The pronouns are also required in questions:

e.g. Wo treffen wir **uns**?

and in orders:

e.g. Setze **dich** hin!
Wascht **euch** die Hände, Kinder!

Dative verbs

Some verbs in German require a *dative* (*indirect*) object where in English there is a *direct* object. Apart from **folgen** and **begegnen** (see note on Perfect with 'sein, p. 138) the following are in common use and should be particularly noted:
antworten, helfen, danken, zuhören, zusehen, glauben*

e.g. Er hilft sein**er** Mutter.
Ich habe **ihm** schon gedankt.
Er antwortete **dem** Lehrer nicht.

The following expressions which require the dative are also very common and should be noted:

Es gefällt **mir** gut/nicht.
Es geht **mir** gut/nicht gut.
Es gehört **mir**.
Es gelingt **mir**, ... zu + *infinitive*.
Es schmeckt **mir** gut/nicht.
Es tut **mir** leid.
Du tust, er/sie tut **mir** leid.
Es tut **mir** weh.
Mir ist kalt/warm.

Imperfect tense

In German the imperfect tense expresses the idea of *was doing* and *used to do*. It can also (unlike the French imperfect) describe single, completed actions in the past, i.e. *did*.

The imperfect of all regular verbs (weak verbs) is formed by adding the following endings to the stem (infinitive minus **-en** or **-n**).

---

* **Glauben** requires the *dative* when it refers to believing a person, not a fact:
e.g. Ich glaube **es** nicht, *but* Ich glaube **dir** nicht.

136

sagen: ich sagte   klingeln: ich
    du sagtest   klingelte *etc.*
    er sagte
    wir sagten
    ihr sagtet
    Sie sagten
    sie sagten

Infinitives ending in **-den** or **-ten** require an extra **e** for ease of pronunciation:
e.g. baden: ich badete
            du badetest, etc.
    arbeiten: ich arbeitete
              du arbeitetest, etc.
Note also: regnen: es regnete.

A number of irregular verbs (mixed verbs) have the weak endings in the imperfect tense. The most common are **haben (ich hatte), wissen (ich wußte), kennen (ich kannte), bringen (ich brachte), rennen (ich rannte)**, and the modals **können (ich konnte), wollen (ich wollte), sollen (ich sollte), müssen (ich mußte), mögen (ich mochte)**, and **dürfen (ich durfte)**.

Note the absence of Umlauts on modal verbs in the imperfect tense.

Most irregular verbs (strong verbs) have an imperfect tense which ends in a consonant in the **ich** form. There is no rule for forming the imperfect of these verbs; they have to be learnt individually. Their pattern is:

sein: ich war   **sprechen**: ich sprach
    du warst   du sprachst
    er war   er sprach
    wir waren   etc.
    ihr wart
    Sie waren
    sie waren

The most common irregular

imperfects are given in the verb tables (pp. 152–4).

Perfect tense

The perfect tense corresponds to the English tenses *I did* and *I have done*. It is made up of two parts; the auxiliary verb **haben** (or **sein** – see p. 138) and a *past participle*.

In simple sentences the past participle stands at the end of the sentence.

The past participle of regular (weak) verbs is formed thus:
suchen → **ge**sucht

For ease of pronunciation **-et** is added when the final consonant is **-t** or **-d**:
arbeiten → **ge**arbeitet
baden → **ge**badet
Note also regnen → **ge**regnet
e.g. Ich **habe** meinen Paß überall
      gesucht.
    Du **hast** den ganzen Abend
      gearbeitet.

Irregular (strong) verbs have past participles which cannot simply be formed from their infinitives; they must be learnt individually:
e.g. sprechen → ich habe
      gesprochen
    singen → ich habe **gesungen**
The most common are listed on pp. 152–4.

Questions are formed by the inversion of the subject and auxiliary verb:
e.g. **Hast du** gehört?

The perfect tense of modal verbs is not normally required to be known at this level as the imperfect can always be used instead, but it may need to be recognized. When a modal verb simply has a direct object, its perfect is straightforward:

Ich **habe** es nicht **gewollt**.
Er **hat** es leider nicht **gekonnt**.

When it has a dependent infinitive, its past participle has the same form as the infinitive:

e.g. Ich **habe** es nicht **machen wollen**.
  Er **hat** es nicht **machen können**.

Inseparable verbs can either be regular (weak) or irregular (strong). Neither add **ge-** to form their past participle. Regular inseparable verbs have the regular **-t** endings:

e.g. verlegen → ich habe **verlegt**.

Irregular past participles have to be learnt:

e.g. verlieren → ich habe **verloren**.

Apart from **verlieren**, all verbs ending in **-ieren** are verbs 'borrowed' from other languages (mainly French and Italian). These are weak verbs, but do not add **ge-** to form their past participle:

e.g. telefonieren → ich habe **telefoniert**.

As separable verbs are made up of recognizable verbs and a separable prefix, the past participle is that of the original verb plus the prefix, all written as one word:

e.g. holen → ich habe **geholt**.
  abholen → ich habe **abgeholt**.

Perfect with 'sein'

In German all intransitive verbs (i.e. those with no direct object) expressing motion or change of state require **sein** and not **haben** as the auxiliary verb in the perfect tense. The past participles of these verbs can be regular or irregular;

their formation and use follow the normal rules (see p. 137).

e.g. eilen: Er **ist** in die Küche **geeilt**.
  gehen: Ich **bin** ins Dorf **gegangen**.

Note also the verbs **sein**, **bleiben** and **werden** which fall into this category:

e.g. Ich **bin** zweimal in Deutschland **gewesen**.
  Ich selbst **bin** zu Hause **geblieben**.
  Er **ist** Lehrer **geworden**.

Some of these verbs can be used transitively or intransitively (i.e. with or without a direct object). When they have a direct object, they are conjugated with **haben**; when they do not, they are conjugated with **sein**:

e.g. Ich **bin** in die Stadt **gefahren**.
  Ich **habe** das Auto in die Stadt **gefahren**.

Some of these verbs, which have a direct object in English, require **sein** in German and are followed by an *indirect object* in the *dative*. Two common examples of this are **folgen** and **begegnen**:

e.g. Ich **bin** mein**em** Freund in der Stadt **begegnet**.
  Der Hund **ist dem** Jung**en** zur Schule **gefolgt**.

Verbs requiring **sein** are indicated in the verb tables (pp. 152–4) and in the end vocabulary.

The pluperfect tense

The *pluperfect* tense expresses the English *had done*. It is formed and follows the same rules as the perfect tense (see p. 137), except that instead of the auxiliary verbs being in the *present* tense, they are in the *imperfect*:

e.g. ich **hatte** gesucht

ich **war** gefahren
ich **hatte** machen müssen.

The future tense

The present tense, combined with a suitable adverb, can be used to talk about the future (like the English 'He is going there tomorrow'):
e.g. Ich **mache** es morgen.
Er **kommt** später.

The true future tense (*I shall*, *you will*, etc.) is formed by using the present tense of **werden** + infinitive. The infinitive stands at the end of the clause:
e.g. Ich **werde** es morgen **machen**.
Wird der Karl auf der Party **sein**?

Lassen + infinitive

Lassen, when used with an infinitive, has the meaning *to get something done*. In the present and imperfect tense **lassen** is regular:
e.g. Ich **lasse** mein Auto reparieren.
Ich **ließ** meinen Ledermantel reinigen.

In the perfect tense, instead of the normal past participle **gelassen**, **lassen** is used. This is similar to the perfect tense of modal verbs (see p. 137):
e.g. Ich **habe** mir die Haare schneiden **lassen**.

Lassen can also, of course, be in the infinitive:
e.g. Ich war krank und **mußte** die Zeitung holen **lassen**.

Zu + infinitive

Apart from the modal verbs, which are followed by a plain infinitive (see p. 138), all other verbs and structures which are followed by an infinitive require the addition of **zu**. Its position in relation to the infinitive is as follows:

(*simple verb*) **zu** kaufen (i.e. before the verb)
(*inseparable verb*) **zu** beginnen (i.e. before the verb)
(*separable verb*) aus**zu**gehen (i.e. between the prefix and the infinitive and written as one word)

The **zu** + *infinitive* stands at the *end* of the sentence, and is separated from the main clause by a comma.
e.g. Ich habe keine Lust, in die Stadt **zu fahren**.
Ich hatte keine Gelegenheit, den Kölner Dom **zu besichtigen**.

In order to ...

In order to ... is expressed in German by **um ... zu** + *infinitive*. Note that **um** stands at the beginning of the clause, **zu** + *infinitive* at the end. The rules for the position of **zu** in relation to the infinitive are given above.
e.g. Ich fahre in die Stadt, **um** ein paar Einkäufe **zu machen**.
Ich gehe in eine Telephonzelle, **um** meine Freundin **anzurufen**.

The **um ... zu** clause is separated from the main clause by a comma.

The conditional tense and the subjunctive

The conditional tense (*I should/ would*, *you would*, etc.) is formed by using the imperfect subjunctive of **werden** with an infinitive. The infinitive stands at the end of the clause.

i.e. ich **würde** + *infinitive*
   du **würdest**
    er **würde**
  wir **würden**
  ihr **würdet**
  Sie **würden**
  sie **würden**

The imperfect subjunctive of other verbs has the same meaning as the conditional, and is frequently found in expressions such as:
Ich **möchte** ...
Könntest du ...?
Wir **sollten** ...
Würden Sie bitte ... ?

Rules for the formation of the subjunctive are not important at this level; the subjunctive of a few important verbs should be learnt. The endings are **-e, -est, -e, -en, -et, -en, -en**.

Apart from the verbs mentioned above, the following are important:
ich würde sein → ich **wäre**
ich würde haben → ich **hätte**

The patterns of conditional sentences is as follows:
Ich **würde** es **kaufen**, wenn ich genug Geld **hätte**.
Hätte ich genug Geld, **würde** ich es kaufen.
Wenn ich genug Geld **hätte**, **würde** ich es kaufen.

Passive

You will not normally be required to be able to use the passive but will probably need to be able to recognize it.

In English the passive is formed by using various tenses of the verb *to be* with the *past participle* (i.e. She is being fetched, I was injured, it has been stolen, etc.). In German the verb **werden** (to become) is used instead of the verb to be:
e.g. Er **wird abgeholt** – *He's being fetched*.
    Ich **wurde verletzt** – *I was injured*.
    Es **ist gestohlen worden** – *It has been stolen*.
Note that **worden**, rather than the regular past participle **geworden** is used in this structure.

Pronouns

Direct and indirect object pronouns

The pronouns which indicate the various persons of the verb are, of course, the subjects of the verb and hence in the *nominative* case. The following are the *accusative* and *dative* pronouns which correspond to them:

nominative	accusative	dative
ich	mich	mir
du	dich	dir
er	ihn	ihm
sie	sie	ihr
es	es	ihm
man	einen	einem
wir	uns	uns
ihr	euch	euch
Sie	Sie	Ihnen
sie	sie	ihnen

These play the same roles in sentences as those explained elsewhere for the accusative and dative of nouns, i.e. *accusative* – direct object and after certain prepositions; *dative* – indirect object and after certain prepositions.

e.g. Accusative:

> Ich sehe **ihn**
> Sie besucht **mich**
> Ich habe **es**
> Ich kenne **sie** nicht
> für **mich**, ohne **ihn**, gegen **uns**

Dative:

> Gib **mir** die Zeitung!
> Wie geht es **Ihnen**?
> Kann ich **dir** etwas anbieten?
> mit **ihm**, zu **ihr**, bei **uns**

Stressed pronouns

A good rule to bear in mind is that „ein" **steht nie allein**, that is to say, you should never use **ein** unless it stands with a noun (**ein Mann, ein Haus**, etc.). When it has to stand on its own, it must have some special endings:

	m	f	n
nom.	ein**er**	ein**e**	ein(**e**)**s**
acc.	ein**en**	ein**e**	ein(**e**)**s**
dat.	ein**em**	ein**er**	ein**em**

You will already have met one of these in counting **eins, zwei, drei,** etc. Here are some more examples:
Wieviele Jungen sind in der Klasse?
– Nur **einer**!
Ein(**e**)**s** von den Mädchen verpaßte den Zug.

These endings also apply to **kein** and all of the possessive adjectives (**mein, dein,** etc.):
Wieviel Geld hast du? Ich habe **kein(e)s**.
Es ist **keiner** da!
Wessen Mantel ist das? **Meiner**.
Mit welchem Wagen fahren wir? Mit **meinem**.

Use of capitals in letter-writing

Sie, Ihnen, and **Ihr(e)** are always written with capital letters; normally **du, dich, dir, dein(e),** and **ihr, euch, euer(e)** are written with small letters. However, when writing letters, cards, etc., they are written with capitals:
e.g. Vielen Dank für **Deinen** Brief.
Ich wünsche **Euch** alles Gute.

Relative pronouns

The relative pronouns (*who, whom, which,* etc.) are, with a few exceptions, the same in German as the definite articles:

	m	f	n	pl
nom. (who, which)	der	die	das	die
acc. (whom, which)	den	die	das	die
gen. (whose, of which)	**dessen**	**deren**	**dessen**	**deren**
dat. (to whom, which)	dem	der	dem	**denen**

The relative pronoun takes its number and gender from the word it refers back to; its case depends on the part it plays in its own clause.

Relative clauses are subordinate clauses, so the finite verb stands at the end of the clause (see p. 143):
e.g. Der Mann, **der** dort **steht**, ist …
Der Mann, **den** du dort **siehst**, ist …
Die Frau, **deren Tochter** krank **ist**, heißt …
Die Frau, **der** er es **gab**, heißt …
Die Kinder, **mit denen** er **spricht**, sind …

141

Note that the relative pronoun cannot be omitted as it can in English:

e.g. The man I saw ...
    Der Mann, **den** ich sah ...

'Was' as a relative

Was is sometimes used as a relative pronoun. Its use in the following cases should be noted:
Alles, was man auf dem Markt kauft, ist billig.
Sie kaufte **nichts, was** sie im Kaufhaus sah.
Das Beste/Einzige, was ich empfehlen kann, ist ...

This, that, this one, that one

This and *that* are expressed in German by, respectively, **dieser/diese/dieses** and **jener/jene/jenes**. However, **jener**, etc. sounds rather old-fashioned and is usually replaced by:
dieser/diese/dieses + *noun* + **dort**
(literally *this ...... there*)
or **der/die/das** + *noun* + **dort**
    (literally *the ...... there*)

e.g. dieser | Mann dort
     der |

Of course **dieser, der**, etc. can be in any case:
Siehst du | dies**en** | Mann dort?
        | d**en** |
Mit | dies**em** | Bus dort ...
   | d**em** |

This one and *that one* are expressed by:
dieser/diese/dieses + **hier** or **dort**

Often they are expressed by:
der/die/das + **hier** or **dort**

When spoken, the **der/die/das** is stressed.

These pronouns can, of course, be in any case:

Welcher Mann?	Dieser Der	hier/dort
Welchen Mann?	Diesen Den	hier/dort
Mit welchem Bus? Mit	diesem dem	hier/dort

Word order

Main clauses

Except in questions, the verb in main clauses is always the *second idea*. In the simplest sentences, of course, the first idea will be the subject of the verb:

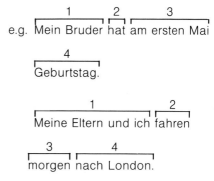

e.g. Mein Bruder hat am ersten Mai Geburtstag.

Meine Eltern und ich fahren morgen nach London.

If any of the other ideas in the sentence are put first, the subject and verb must be inverted to keep the verb as the second idea:

e.g. Am ersten Mai hat mein Bruder Geburtstag.

142

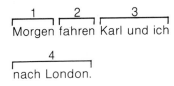

Morgen fahren Karl und ich

nach London.

Note that **ja**, **doch**, **nein** and exclamations such as **ach!** are considered as being separate from the rest of the sentence. They do not affect the word order:

e.g. Ja, ich bin sehr müde.
Ach! das tut mir leid.

Coordinating conjunctions

Conjunctions are words which join clauses together. In German, some conjunctions, called *co-ordinating conjunctions*, do not affect the word order in the second clause (i.e. the verb remains the second idea).
The most common of these are:

und and
denn for, because
oder or
aber but
sondern but

e.g. Ich stand zu spät auf, und **ich verpaßte** den Bus.
Er kann nicht in die Schule, denn **er ist** zu krank.

Although **aber** and **sondern** both mean *but*, they have different uses. **Aber** means *but* in the sense of *however*; **sondern** means *but* in the sense of *on the contrary*; it can only be used when all of the following conditions are fulfilled:

— the first statement is in the negative;
— the second statement contradicts the first;
— both statements have the same subject.

e.g. Ich bin ziemlich dumm, **aber** meine Schwester ist intelligent.
Ich bin nicht intelligent, **sondern** ich bin sehr dumm.

When the subordinate clause stands before the main clause, it affects the word order in the same way that any other 'idea' does, i.e. the subject and verb must be inverted to keep the finite verb as the second idea:
e.g. Ich bleibe zu Hause, wenn es regnet.

but Wenn es regnet, **bleibe ich** zu Hause.

Subordinate clauses

Other conjunctions (subordinating conjunctions) change the word order in the clauses they introduce. The most common are:

daß that
ob whether
als as, when
wenn if, whenever
bis until
weil because
bevor before
nachdem after
während while
obgleich/obwohl although
damit so that, in order that
(so) daß with the result that

These subordinating conjunctions send the finite verb to the end of the clause they introduce:
e.g. Er weiß noch nicht, **daß** ich da bin.
Ich weiß nicht, **ob** ich mitkommen kann.
Er kommt, **obwohl** er einen Unfall gehabt hat.

Note that, when a separable verb is involved, the verb goes to the end of the clause and is written together with the prefix:
e.g. Mein Vater **kommt** bald **zurück**.

143

Ich warte, bis mein Vater **zurückkommt**.

In subordinate clauses introduced by an interrogative (i.e. question word) after phrases such as 'I don't know ...' and 'Could you tell me ... ?' the finite verb stands at the end of the clause. The interrogatives (question words) with which they start are the same as the normal interrogatives:
e.g. **Wo** sind deine Eltern?
Ich weiß nicht, **wo** sie **sind**.
Wann machen die Banken auf?
Können Sie mir sagen, **wann** die Banken **aufmachen?**

When there is no question word in the original question (i.e. *'Have you ... ?' 'Can I ... ?'*), **ob** (= *if, whether*) is used to introduce the clause:
e.g. Kommt der Karl auch mit?
Ich weiß nicht, **ob** er mitkommt.

Wann, wenn, als

Wann, **wenn** and **als** all mean 'when' and can all introduce subordinate clauses. They are used in different situations, however.

If *when* can be replaced by *at what time* then **wann** should be used:
e.g. Ich weiß nicht, **wann** der Film beginnt (i.e. *at what time* it begins)

If *when* can be replaced by *whenever* then **wenn** should be used:
e.g. Ich sehe fern, **wenn** ich nichts Besseres zu tun habe (i.e. *whenever* I haven't anything better to do)
Note that **wenn** can also mean *if*.

When *one occasion in the past* is being referred to **als** should be used:
e.g. **Als** er aus dem Kino kam, ging er ins Restaurant (i.e. he came out of the cinema *on one occasion*)

Direct and indirect objects

The following sentences illustrate the rules for word order when a sentence contains both a direct and an indirect object:
Der Mann gibt **seiner Frau den Brief**.
(i.e. when two nouns – indirect before direct)
Der Mann gibt **ihn seiner Frau**.
Der Mann gibt **ihr den Brief**.
(i.e. when a pronoun and a noun – pronoun before noun)
Der Mann gibt **ihn ihr**.
(i.e. when two pronouns – direct before indirect)

Time, manner, place

When a sentence includes more than one adverb, or adverbial phrase, they must follow the order *Time* (i.e. when?), *Manner* (i.e. how?), *Place* (i.e. where? where to? where from?):

e.g. Ich fahre morgen mit dem Zug nach Köln.

Negatives

The negative (*not*) is usually expressed by **nicht**:
e.g. Er ist **nicht** alt.
Ich sehe Karl **nicht**.
Ich habe **nicht** im September Geburtstag.

When a noun is being made negative (*not a ..., no ..., not any*

...) then **kein(e)** is used. **Kein(e)** follows the pattern of **ein(e)**. Its plural form is **keine**.

e.g. Das ist **kein** Problem.
Ich habe **keine** Geschwister.

A useful tip is to avoid the combination **nicht + ein(e)**. Use **kein(e)**!

Prepositions

Prepositions with the accusative

Apart from indicating the direct object of the verb, the accusative (**den**, **die**, **das**, etc.) is used after certain prepositions. The most common are:

für for
durch through
ohne without
um around
gegen against
bis an up to
entlang* along

e.g. **für meinen** Bruder
durch den Wald
um die Ecke

Prepositions with the dative

The most common prepositions which always take the dative are:
aus out of, from
bei at _____'s house, shop
mit with
nach after, to
seit since

von from
zu to
gegenüber* opposite

e.g. **aus dem** Haus
mit meiner Freundin
nach der Schule

The following contractions are usually made:
zu dem → **zum**
zu der → **zur**
bei dem → **beim**
von dem → **vom**

Notice also the expression **an** + *dative* **vorbei** which means 'past':
e.g. **am** Bahnhof **vorbei**.

Prepositions with the accusative and the dative

Certain prepositions take either the accusative or the dative according to their meaning. With the *dative* they answer the question **wo**? and tell you where something or someone is. With the *accusative* they answer the question **wohin**? and tell you where something or someone is going or moving to.

in in; into
an at, on; up to, over to, on to
auf on; on to
hinter behind; (going) behind
vor in front of; (going) in front of
unter under; (going) under
über above, over; (going) over, across
zwischen between; (going) between
neben near, next to, beside; (down) beside, next to

---

* **Entlang** usually follows the noun, e.g. Er geht **die Straße entlang**.

* **Gegenüber** usually follows the noun, e.g. **dem Bahnhof gegenüber**.

Karl ist **im** Garten *but* Er geht **in den** Garten.
Es steht **auf dem** Boden *but* Es fällt **auf den** Boden.
Er steht **am** Fenster *but* Er geht **ans** Fenster.

Note the following contractions:
in dem → **im**   an dem → **am**
in das → **ins**   an das → **ans**

There are many cases where German is far more accurate than English in its application of **wohin**?, answered using one of the above prepositions with the accusative. Here are a few examples:

Wohin hängt er seinen Mantel? – in **den** Schrank/in **die** Ecke/hinter **die** Tür.
Wohin schreibt er? – In **ein** Heft/an **die** Tafel.
Wohin setzt er sich? – In **den** Lehnstuhl/auf**s** Sofa/neben **mich**.

Compare these with the following:
Wo hängt sein Mantel? – **Im** Schrank/in **der** Ecke/hinter **der** Tür.
Wo steht die Übung? – **Im** Heft/an **der** Tafel.
Wo sitzt er? – **Im** Lehnstuhl/auf **dem** Sofa/neben **mir**.

Prepositions with the genitive

Some prepositions are followed by the genitive case. Some common ones are:
trotz, wegen, während, statt, außerhalb, innerhalb
e.g. während meines kurzen Aufenthalt(e)s; trotz des schlechten Wetters; wegen* seiner Krankheit

---

* **Wegen** can precede or follow the noun i.e. **wegen seiner Krankheit** or **seiner Krankheit wegen**.

Prepositional objects

Some verbs are associated with certain prepositions; they are said to have prepositional objects. Unfortunately the prepositions are often quite different from their English equivalents and need to be learnt carefully along with the cases they require. The following are very common:

denken an + accusative
   to think of (i.e. have in mind)
halten von + dative
   to think of (i.e. to rate)
warten auf + accusative
   to wait for
bitten um + accusative
   to ask for (i.e. request)
fragen nach + dative
   to ask about (i.e. to make enquiries about)
ankommen in + dative
   to arrive in, at
vorbeigehen an }
vorbeifahren an } + dative
   to go past
Angst haben vor + dative
   to be afraid of
sich freuen auf + accusative
   to look forward to
sich freuen über + accusative
   to be happy about
sich erinnern an + accusative
   to remember
schreiben an + accusative
   to write to

e.g. Du solltest **an deine** Eltern **denken**.
   Was **hältst** du **von meiner** Jacke?
   Darf ich **um** Feuer **bitten**? *etc.*

Notice how, when things rather than people are referred to, a special interrogative (question word) is used,

formed from **wo-** or **wor-** + a preposition, instead of a preposition + **wen**? or **wem**?:
e.g. **Auf wen** wartest du?
   (i.e. *who(m)?*)
   Worauf wartest du? (i.e. *what?*)
   An wen denkst du?
   (i.e. *who(m)?*)
   Woran denkst du? (i.e. *what?*)

A similar difference is found when these verbs are used with a pronoun; when referring to things, pronouns are formed from **da-** or **dar-** + a preposition:
e.g. Ich warte jetzt **auf ihn**.
   (i.e. *person*)
   Ich warte jetzt **darauf**. (i.e. *thing*)
   Ich denke oft **an sie**.
   (i.e. *person*)
   Ich denke oft **daran**. (i.e. *thing*)

Adjectives

Possessive adjectives

Possessive adjectives (*my, your*, etc.) follow the pattern of **ein**, **eine**, **ein**. They are as follows:

m	f	n	pl	
mein	meine	mein	meine	*my*
dein	deine	dein	deine	*your*
sein	seine	sein	seine	*his*
ihr	ihre	ihr	ihre	*her*
unser	unsere	unser	unsere	*our*
eu(e)r	eu(e)re	eu(e)r	eu(e)re	*your*
Ihr	Ihre	Ihr	Ihre	*your*
ihr	ihre	ihr	ihre	*their*

Comparative of adjectives

Regular adjectives form the comparative, as in English, by adding **-er**. In German an Umlaut (¨) is also added wherever possible:
e.g. klein → klein**er**
   groß → gr**ö**ß**er**

Note these irregular comparatives:
gut → besser
viel → mehr
hoch → höher

The comparison is made with **als**:
e.g. Ich bin kleiner **als** er.
   Er ist größer **als** mein Bruder.

Note that both people or things being compared are in the same case (i.e. the nominative).

Superlative of adjectives

The superlative form of German adjectives is similar to the form used in English: **-st** or **-est*** is added to the original adjective and an Umlaut is usually added wherever possible:
e.g. klein → kleiner → **kleinst-**
   jung → jünger → **jüngst-**
   alt → älter → **ältest-**

Since the superlative will normally be used with the definite article (the biggest, the smallest, etc.) the appropriate adjectival ending must be used (see note below on adjectival endings):
e.g. **das** jüngst**e** Kind, **die** ältest**e** Frau, etc.

The following irregular superlatives should be noted:
groß → größer → **größt-**
gut → besser → **best-**
hoch → höher → **höchst-**
nah → näher → **nächst-**
viel → mehr → **meist-**

---

* Adjectives ending in **-d**, **-s**, **-ß**, **-sch**, **-t**, or **-tz** end in **-est**.

There are times when the superlative of an adjective has the meaning 'at its best', 'at one's tiredest', 'at their most beautiful', etc. This is expressed by the German **am besten**, **am müdesten**, **am schönsten**, etc.

Adjectival endings

When an adjective and the noun it describes are separated by a verb, the adjective does not change:
Karl ist **groß**.
Die Kinder werden **groß**.

However, when an adjective stands next to a noun, certain endings must be added to the adjective according to the gender and the case of the noun. These endings need to be learnt carefully and are set out in the tables on pp. 150–1.

Adjectives used as nouns

A number of adjectives can be used to form nouns. They start, of course, with a capital letter, and require adjectival endings of the kind mentioned above:
e.g. deutsch → **ein** Deutsch**er** – a German
alt → **ein** Alt**er** – an old man, etc.

A typical example of this kind of noun is given in full in the table on pp. 150–1. Nouns which follow this pattern are indicated in the end vocabulary.

Etwas/nichts/wenig/viel + adjective

Etwas and **nichts** are invariable, i.e. they always remain the same. So, too, are **wenig** and **viel** in the singular. However, when they are followed by an adjective (*something cheap*, *nothing interesting*, etc.), the adjective must have a strong neuter ending. In most cases the adjective is written with a capital letter. Although separate genitive and dative forms exist, they are not likely to be needed:
e.g. Es gibt **etwas Interessantes** im Fernsehen.
Er hat **nichts Wichtiges** gesagt.
Es gab **viel/wenig Preiswertes** auf dem Markt.

Ander is a common exception to the capital letter rule:
Ich will etwas **anderes**.
Haben Sie nichts **anderes**?

Comparative adjectives can be used in the same way:
e.g. Haben Sie nichts **Billigeres/Besseres**?

Adverbs

Formation

Most German adjectives can be used as adverbs without any alteration being made to them:
e.g. Sie ist **schön**, *but also*: Sie singt **schön**.
Ein **schneller** Schwimmer, *but also*: Er schwimmt **schnell**.
Sometimes this sounds wrong to English ears:
Er ist ein **guter** Schwimmer, *but also*: Er schwimmt **gut**.

Comparison of adverbs

The comparative of adverbs is formed in exactly the same way as adjectives (see p. 147).
e.g. Er singt **schöner** als sie.
Ich laufe **schneller** als er.

Superlative of adverbs

The superlative form of the adverb is the same as the alternative superlative form for adjectives explained on p. 148:

e.g. Sie singt **am schönsten**.
Ich laufe **am schnellsten**.

The following common irregular adverbs should be noted:

bald → **früher** → **am frühesten**
gern → **lieber** → **am liebsten**
gut → **besser** → **am besten**
viel ⎫
　　⎬ → **mehr** → **am meisten**
sehr ⎭

Miscellaneous

Jobs and nationalities

When speaking about people's jobs and nationalities it is usual to omit **ein(e)**:

e.g. Mein Vater ist **Briefträger**.
Ich bin **Engländer(in)**.
Sie sind **Deutsche**, *etc.*

However, **ein(e)** is included when there is an adjective with the noun:

e.g. Er ist **ein guter Lehrer**.
Sie ist **keine gute Lehrerin**.

Use of ß

Most examination boards make the use of **ß** optional. However, for reference, the following rules apply.

ß is used:
— at the end of a word e.g. **Fuß, muß**.
— before the letter **t** e.g. **heißt, ißt**.
— after a long vowel e.g. **heiße, große**.
In all other cases **ss** is used.

Expressions of quantity

Expressions of quantity which require *of* in English (a bottle *of*, a pound *of*, etc.) do not require an equivalent preposition in German:

e.g. Ich kaufe eine Flasche Wein, ein Pfund Hackfleisch und 250 Gramm Bierwurst.
20 Liter Super, bitte!

Accusative in time expressions

In German the accusative is usually used to express the length of time something goes on for, i.e. answering the question **wie lange**?

e.g. Wie lange warst du dort?
Ich war **einige Stunden/den ganzen Abend/einen Monat/ein ganzes Wochenende** dort.

Most of/both of

The expressions *most of* and *both of* are both adjectives in German, **meist-** and **beid-**; consequently they must have the appropriate adjectival endings (see pp. 150–1).

e.g. most of the time, **die meiste Zeit**
most of the schoolchildren, **die meisten Schüler**
both children, **die beiden** ⎫ **Kinder**
　　　　　　　　 beide ⎭

Genitive expressing indefinite times

The genitive case is often used to express indefinite time; this is the equivalent of the kind of expressions one hears in certain English dialects ('I go(es) there *of a Saturday* afternoon').

One way it is used is to refer to a particular, but unspecified, time, i.e.

'one day', 'one morning', etc.:
eines Tages, eines Morgens, eines Nachmittags, eines Abends
These expressions can include an adjective:
Eines bitterkalten Dezemberabend**s** ...

Eines herrlichen Sommertag**es** ...

It can also be used with parts of the day to indicate when something occurred, either once or regularly, i.e. 'in the morning', 'every morning':
morgens, vormittags, nachmittags, abends, nachts
These are adverbs and therefore do not have capital letters.
The last of these, which means 'in the night', 'at night', is not the grammatically correct genitive form of **die Nacht**, but is formed by analogy with the others.

The genitive is also used in similar fashion with the days of the week, meaning 'on Monday(s)', 'every Monday', etc.:
montags, dienstags, mittwochs, etc.

Apposition

When a noun stands in apposition to another (i.e. stands next to it to give more information about it) it must be in the *same case* as the first noun:
e.g. **Herr** Schmidt, **der** Schulleiter, ist krank.

Kennen Sie **Herrn** Schmidt, **unseren** Schulleiter?
Das ist das Haus **meines** Freunde**s**, **des** Deutschlehrer**s**.
Er spricht mit **seiner** Freundin, **der** Ärztin.

Ago

The idea of *ago* is expressed in German by using the preposition **vor** + *dative*.
e.g. **vor einer** Woche
vor drei Jahr**en**, etc.

Seit wann?

One way of expressing in German *how long* someone has been doing something (e.g. I have been waiting for an hour, living here for ten years, etc.) is to use the *present tense* with **seit** + dative (literally 'I am _____ing since' + a certain length of time).

Questions about this are also framed in the present tense:
e.g. Seit wann **lernst** du Deutsch?
Ich **lerne** es schon seit drei Jahren.
Seit wann **wartest** du?
Ich **warte** erst seit fünf Minuten.
Ich **warte** seit fast einer halben Stunde.

Noun declensions and adjectival endings

Masculine (strong)

N	der Mann	die Männer
A	den Mann	die Männer
G	des Mannes	der Männer
D	dem Mann	den Männern

Masculine (weak)

	der Junge	die Jungen
	den Jungen	die Jungen
	des Jungen	der Jungen
	dem Jungen	den Jungen

	Feminine		**Feminine**		**Neuter**	
N	die Frau	die Frauen	die Stadt	die Städte	das Haus	die Häuser
A	die Frau	die Frauen	die Stadt	die Städte	das Haus	die Häuser
G	der Frau	der Frauen	der Stadt	der Städte	des Hauses	der Häuser
D	der Frau	den Frauen	der Stadt	den Städten	dem Haus	den Häusern.

Adjectives used as nouns

N	der Deutsche	ein Deutscher
A	den Deutschen	einen Deutschen
G	des Deutschen	eines Deutschen
D	dem Deutschen	einem Deutschen

N	die Deutsche	eine Deutsche
A	die Deutsche	eine Deutsche
G	der Deutschen	einer Deutschen
D	der Deutschen	einer Deutschen

N	die Deutschen	Deutsche
A	die Deutschen	Deutsche
G	der Deutschen	Deutscher
D	den Deutschen	Deutschen

Adjectives after ein, eine, ein; dieser, diese, dieses, etc.

N	der junge Mann	die schöne Frau	das kleine Haus
A	den jungen Mann	die schöne Frau	das kleine Haus
G	des jungen Mannes	der schönen Frau	des kleinen Hauses
D	dem jungen Mann	der schönen Frau	dem kleinen Haus

N	die jungen Leute
A	die jungen Leute
G	der jungen Leute
D	den jungen Leuten

Adjectives after der, die, das; kein, keine, kein, etc.

N	ein junger Mann	eine schöne Frau	ein kleines Haus
A	einen jungen Mann	eine schöne Frau	ein kleines Haus
G	eines jungen Mannes	einer schönen Frau	eines kleinen Hauses
D	einem jungen Mann	einer schönen Frau	einem kleinen Haus

Adjectives standing on their own in front of a noun

N	deutscher Wein	deutsche Butter	deutsches Bier	deutsche Würste
A	deutschen Wein	deutsche Butter	deutsches Bier	deutsche Würste
G	deutschen Weines	deutscher Butter	deutschen Bieres	deutscher Würste
D	deutschem Wein	deutscher Butter	deutschem Bier	deutschen Würsten

Irregular verbs

The following list includes all the irregular verbs which occur in the book. Meanings and other relevant details are given in the end vocabulary and an asterisk refers the student to this list. Where not specifically given, compound nouns should be deduced from the simple form, e.g. **abbiegen** from **biegen**; **verbringen** from **bringen**; **verstehen** from **stehen**, etc.

Infinitive	Irreg. present	Imperfect	Perfect
beginnen		begann	hat begonnen
beißen		biß	hat gebissen
betrügen		betrog	hat betrogen
biegen		bog	hat gebogen
bieten		bot	hat geboten
binden		band	hat gebunden
bitten		bat	hat gebeten
blasen	bläst	blies	hat geblasen
bleiben		blieb	ist geblieben
brechen	bricht	brach	hat gebrochen
brennen		brannte	hat gebrannt
bringen		brachte	hat gebracht
denken		dachte	hat gedacht
dürfen*	darf, darfst, darf	durfte	hat gedurft / dürfen
empfehlen	empfiehlt	empfahl	hat empfohlen
essen	ißt	aß	hat gegessen
fahren	fährt	fuhr	ist gefahren
fallen	fällt	fiel	ist gefallen
fangen	fängt	fing	hat gefangen
finden		fand	hat gefunden
fliegen		flog	ist geflogen
fließen		floß	ist geflossen
fliehen		floh	ist geflohen
frieren		fror	hat gefroren
geben	gibt	gab	hat gegeben
gehen		ging	ist gegangen
gelingen		gelang	ist gelungen
gelten	gilt	galt	hat gegolten
genießen		genoß	hat genossen

* The past participles of auxiliary verbs of mood (**dürfen**, **mögen**, **müssen**, **wollen**, **sollen**) is replaced by its infinitive when immediately preceded by an infinitive. This is also true of **lassen**. e.g. Er **hat** es **gedurft** *but* Er **hat** nicht **mitgehen dürfen**

Infinitive	Irreg. present	Imperfect	Perfect
geschehen	geschieht	geschah	ist geschehen
gewinnen		gewann	hat gewonnen
graben	gräbt	grub	hat gegraben
greifen		griff	hat gegriffen
haben	habe, hast, hat	hatte	hat gehabt
halten	hält	hielt	hat gehalten
hängen		hing	hat gehangen
heben		hob	hat gehoben
heißen		hieß	hat geheißen
helfen	hilft	half	hat geholfen
kennen		kannte	hat gekannt
kommen		kam	ist gekommen
können	kann, kannst, kann	konnte	hat gekonnt / können
laden	lädt	lud	hat geladen
lassen	läßt	ließ	hat gelassen
laufen	läuft	lief	ist gelaufen
leiden		litt	hat gelitten
leihen		lieh	hat geliehen
lesen	liest	las	hat gelesen
liegen		lag	hat gelegen
lügen		log	hat gelogen
meiden		mied	hat gemieden
mißlingen		mißlang	ist mißlungen
mögen	mag, magst, mag	mochte	hat gemocht / mögen
müssen	muß, mußt, muß	mußte	hat gemußt / müssen
nehmen	nimmt	nahm	hat genommen
nennen		nannte	hat genannt
raten	rät	riet	hat geraten
reißen		riß	hat gerissen
reiten		ritt	ist geritten
rennen		rannte	ist gerannt
rufen		rief	hat gerufen
saugen	säugt	sog	hat gesogen
scheiden		schied	hat geschieden
scheinen		schien	hat geschienen
schlafen	schläft	schlief	hat geschlafen
schlagen	schlägt	schlug	hat geschlagen

153

Infinitive	Irreg. present	Imperfect	Perfect
schließen		schloß	hat geschlossen
schneiden		schnitt	hat geschnitten
schreiben		schrieb	hat geschrieben
schreien		schrie	hat geschrien
sehen	sieht	sah	hat gesehen
sein	bin, bist, ist	war	ist gewesen
senden		sandte	hat gesandt
sitzen		saß	hat gesessen
sollen	soll, sollst, soll	sollte	hat gesollt / sollen
sprechen	spricht	sprach	hat gesprochen
stehen		stand	hat gestanden
stehlen	stiehlt	stahl	hat gestohlen
steigen		stieg	ist gestiegen
sterben	stirbt	starb	ist gestorben
stoßen	stößt	stieß	hat gestoßen
streichen		strich	hat gestrichen
tragen	trägt	trug	hat getragen
treffen	trifft	traf	hat getroffen
treiben		trieb	hat getrieben
treten	tritt	trat	ist getreten
trinken		trank	hat getrunken
tun		tat	hat getan
überwinden		überwand	hat überwunden
vergessen	vergißt	vergaß	hat vergessen
verlieren		verlor	hat verloren
verschwinden		verschwand	ist verschwunden
verzeihen		verzieh	hat verziehen
wachsen	wächst	wuchs	ist gewachsen
waschen	wäscht	wusch	hat gewaschen
weisen		wies	hat gewiesen
wenden		wandte	hat gewandt
werden	werde, wirst, wird	wurde	ist geworden
werfen	wirft	warf	hat geworfen
wiegen		wog	hat gewogen
wissen	weiß, weißt, weiß	wußte	hat gewußt
ziehen		zog	hat gezogen

German – English vocabulary

This vocabulary contains all but the most common words which appear in the book. Where a word has several meanings, only those which occur in the book are given.

Verbs marked * are irregular; they, or their root verbs, can be found in the verb lists on pp. 152–4. Verbs marked with † are conjugated with **sein** in the perfect tense. Nouns marked ‡ are weak masculine nouns; those marked § are adjectives used as nouns (see p. 150 for full declensions). F. indicates a familiar or slang word or expression. Plurals are only given where they might be useful.

If you cannot find a compound noun under its initial letter, try looking up the last part(s) of the word:

e.g. **Rotkohl → Kohl; Fußballmannschaft → Mannschaft.**

If you cannot find a word beginning with or containing **ge-,** it is probably a past participle and should be looked up under its infinitive:

e.g. **ausgerutscht → ausrutschen; schiefgegangen → schiefgehen.**

If you cannot find a word beginning with **un-,** look it up under its positive form: e.g. **unangenehm → angenehm; unzufrieden → zufrieden.**

ab, from; **ab sofort**, as of now
die **Abbildung**, illustration
abdrucken, to print
der **Abflug**, take-off
das **Abgas** (-e), exhaust fumes
abgelegen, remote
abgesprochen, agreed
abholen, to fetch, pick up
das **Abitur**, school-leaving exam similar to A level)
ablaufen*†, to go off
ablehnen, to turn down, decline
ablenken, to distract; **sich ablenken**, to take one's mind off things
abschleppen, to tow away
der **Abstellplatz**, (bicycle) park
das **Abteil** (-e), compartment
die **Abteilung** (-en), department
achten auf, to keep an eye on, look after
die **Ahnung**, idea, notion, inkling
die **Aktentasche,** briefcase
alle, all gone
alleinstehend, living alone

allenfalls, if need be; at most; at best
allmählich, gradually
also, thus, therefore; well
das **Alter**, age
anbieten*, to offer
das **Andenken** (-), souvenir
andrücken, to push to
der **Anfang**, beginning
anfänglich, initial(ly)
die **Anfrage**, inquiry
das **Angebot**, offer
angehen*†, to concern
angenehm, pleasant
der **Angestellte** §, employee
angreifen*, to attack
Angst: Angst haben, to be afraid
sich **angurten**, to fasten one's seat belt
anhaben*, to have on, be wearing
anhalten*, to stop
(sich) **anhören**, to listen to
ankommen*†, to arrive; **das kommt darauf an**, that depends

Anlage: in der Anlage,
enclosed
anlegen, to put on
sich **anmelden**, to announce one's
arrival, book in
annehmen*, to accept; assume
anpflanzen, to plant
anprobieren, to try on
anrufen*, to phone, call up
anschauen, to look at
anschließend, following,
ensuing; afterwards
die **Anschlußstelle**, junction
anschreien*, to shout, yell at
die **Ansichtskarte** (-n), postcard
anspannen, to tense (muscles)
sich **anstellen**, to queue (up)
anstrengend, strenuous,
exhausting
die **Anzeige** (-n), advertisement
anziehen*, to put on
(clothes); **sich anziehen***, to
get dressed
der **Anzug** (⁻e), suit
anzünden, to light
die **Apotheke**, chemist's shop
der **Apotheker**, (dispensing) chemist
arbeitslos, unemployed
der **Ärger**, anger; trouble
ärgerlich, annoyed, cross;
annoying
sich **ärgern**, to get annoyed, angry
die **Arznei**, medicine
der **Arzt** (⁻e), **die Ärztin** (-nen),
doctor
der **Aschenbecher** (-), ashtray
atemlos, out of breath
atmen, to breathe
aufblasen*, to blow up,
inflate
aufbringen*, to raise (money)
der **Aufenthalt**, stay
die **Auffahrt**, ascent; approach
road, drive
der **Auffahrunfall**, collision
auffallen*†, to stand out,
attract attention

sich **aufhalten***, to stop, stay
aufhören, to stop, cease
sich **aufklären**, to clear, brighten up
aufleuchten, to light up
aufmachen, to open
aufmerksam, attentive,
observant; **aufmerksam
machen**, to draw someone's
attention to
aufmuntern, to cheer up
aufpassen auf, to look after,
keep an eye on
aufregend, exciting
sich **aufrichten**, to stand, sit up
aufschlagen*, to open; put
up, pitch
aufschlitzen, to slit (open)
**aufsetzen: dem Ganzen die
Krone aufsetzen**, to top it all
aufstehen*†, to stand, get up
der **Aufstieg**, climb, ascent
der **Augenblick** (-e), moment
ausatmen, to breathe out,
exhale
ausbürsten, to brush (out)
sich **ausdenken***, to think up, devise
ausfallen*†, to fail; be cancelled
ausfindig: ausfindig machen,
to find, trace
der **Ausflug** (⁻e), trip, excursion
der **Ausflugswagen**, (excursion)
bus, coach
die **Ausgabe**, distribution, giving
out; counter; edition, issue;
Ausgaben (pl) expenditure,
expenses
der **Ausgang**, way out
ausgeben*, to spend (money)
ausgeglichen, well-balanced
(character)
ausgerechnet, ... of all ...
(e.g. **ausgerechnet mir**, to
me of all people; **ausgerechnet
das,** that of all things)
ausgeschlossen, impossible,
out of the question
aushalten*: es nicht

aushalten*, not to be able to stand it (any longer)

auskommen*†: **gut auskommen mit**, to get on well with

die **Auskunft**, information

das **Ausland**, abroad

ausmachen, to matter

ausnahmsweise, exceptionally, for a change

der **Auspuff**, exhaust

die **Ausrede** (-n), excuse

ausreichend, enough

sich **ausruhen**, to rest

ausrüsten, to fit, equip

ausrutschen†, to slip

die **Aussage** (-n), announcement, statement

sich **ausschlafen***, to have a good sleep

aussehen*, to look, appear

außer, except

äußerst, extremely

aussteigen*†, to climb, get out

ausstellen: einen Strafzettel ausstellen, to write out a (traffic) ticket

ausstoßen*, to utter (cry), heave (sigh)

der **Austausch**, exchange

austragen*, to deliver

auswandern†, to emigrate

ausziehen*, to take off (clothes); **sich ausziehen**, to get undressed

die **Autobahn** (-en), motorway

der **Automat**‡ (-en), (vending) machine

backen*, to bake

baden, to bathe

das **Badetuch** (¨er), towel

der **Bahnhof** (¨e), station

der **Bahnsteig** (-e), platform

bald, soon

Bau: auf dem Bau, in the building trade

bauen, to build

der **Bauer** (-n)‡, farmer

die **Baustelle**, building site

der **Beamte** § (-n), **die Beamtin** (-nen), official

beauftragen, to instruct

bedeckt, covered

bedeuten, to mean

die **Bedienung**, service

Bedienungshinweise (pl), instructions

sich **beeilen**, to hurry, get a move on

sich **befinden***, to be, find oneself, be found, situated

begegnen†, to meet, bump into

beginnen*, to begin, start

die **Begleitung**, company

begrüßen, to greet, welcome

behalten*, to keep; **im Auge behalten***, to keep an eye on

behandeln, to treat

behaupten, to claim, maintain, assert

der **Beifahrer** (-), passenger

das **Bein** (-e), leg

beinahe, almost, very nearly

beißen*, to bite

sich **beklagen**, to complain

bekommen*, to get, obtain

beliebt, popular, well-liked

bellen, to bark

belohnen, to reward

bemerken, to notice

beneiden, to envy

benötigen, to need

benutzen, benützen, to use

das **Benzin**, petrol

beobachten, to observe, watch

bequem, comfortable (-ly)

beraten*, to advise

der **Berater**, advisor

bereit, ready, prepared

der **Berg**, mountain, hill

157

die **Bergkuppe**, (round) mountain top
der **Bericht**, report
der **Beruf**, job, occupation
berufstätig, working, in work
beruhigen, to calm, quieten, soothe, comfort
beschäftigt, busy
beschließen*, to decide
beschreiben*, to describe
besetzt, occupied, taken
besichtigen, to visit, have a look at, view, tour
die **Besichtigungsfahrt**, sight-seeing tour
die **Besichtigungszeiten**, hours of opening
besitzen*, to own, possess
der **Besitzer** (-), owner
besonders, especially; **nichts Besonder(e)s**, nothing much, in particular, special
besorgen, to get, acquire
besorgt, anxious, concerned
besprechen*, to discuss
bestehen*, to exist, be in existence; pass (exam); **bestehen auf**, to insist upon; **bestehen aus**, to consist of, comprise
bestimmt, certain(ly), definite(ly); **bestimmt für**, intended for
bestrafen, to punish
besuchen, to visit; attend
betragen*, to amount, come to
betreffen*, to concern
Betrieb: außer Betrieb, out of order
betrügen*, to deceive, cheat
beunruhigend, worrying
bevorstehen*, to be imminent, near
beweisen*, to prove
bewundern, to admire
bewußt, conscious, aware

bezahlen, to pay (for)
bezw., beziehungsweise, or, respectively
biegen*, to bend
bieten*, to offer
das **Bild** (-er), picture, photo(graph)
bilden, to form
billig, cheap
binden*, to tie, bind
bis, until
bisher, up to now, hitherto
bitten*, to ask, beg
das **Blatt** (-er), leaf; sheet
bleiben*†, to stay, remain
der **Blick**, glance
blöd, silly, stupid
bloß, simply, merely
die **Blutprobe**, blood test
der **Boden**, ground; floor; **zu Boden**, on(to) the ground, floor
böse, angry
die **Botschaft**, embassy
brauchen, to need
die **BRD** (**Bundesrepublik Deutschland**), German Federal Republic, West Germany
brechen*, to break
die **Bremse** (-n), brake
bremsen, to brake
brennen*, to burn
das **Brett** (-er), board
die **Briefmarke** (-n), (postage) stamp
der **Brief** (-e), letter
die **Brieftasche** (-n), wallet
die **Brille**, (pair of) glasses, spectacles
bringen*, to bring
die **Brombeere** (-n), blackberry
bummeln, to stroll, wander
der **Bummelstreik**, go-slow
Bundes-, Federal
das **Bundesgebiet**, federal territory (i.e. West Germany)

die **Burg** (-en), castle
der **Bürger** (-), citizen
der **Bürgermeister**, mayor

die **Clique**, group, gang
die **CSSR**, Czechoslovakia

dabei, there
dagegen, against it; on the
other hand
damit, with it; so that
der **Dampfer**, steamer
die **Dampferfahrt**, boat trip
darauf, on it; **kurz darauf**,
shortly afterwards
darin, in it
dauern, to last
die **Dauerstellung**, long-term job
sich **davonmachen**, to make off,
run away
dazu, in addition, as well; for
that
dazukommen*†, to arrive (on
the scene); be added, follow
die **DB** (**Deutsche Bundesbahn**),
Federal Railways
die **DDR** (**Deutsche
Demokratische Republik**),
German Democratic
Republic, East Germany
der **Deckel**, lid, top
denken*, to think
das **Denkmal** (¨er), monument
deren, whose
deshalb, therefore
dessen, whose
deswegen, therefore
deutlich, clear(ly)
das **Dia** (-s), slide
dicht, thick, dense, heavy
der **Dieb** (-e), **die Diebin** (-nen),
thief
der **Diebstahl**, theft
Dienst: im Dienst, on duty
der **Dom**, cathedral
doof, F. daft

das **Dorf** (¨er), village
dort, there; **dorther**, from
there; **dorthin**, (to) there
das **Dragée** (-s), (sugar-coated)
pill, tablet
(sich) **drehen**, to turn
dringend, urgent, pressing
das **Drittel**, third
die **Drogerie**, chemist's shop
drücken, to push, press
dummerweise, foolishly,
stupidly; unfortunately
dunkel, dark
dünn thin; **dünn gesät**, few
and far between
durchblättern, to leaf, flick
through
durchfallen*†, to fail (exam)
Durchgang: kein Durchgang!
no right of way
durchgehend, continuous(ly),
round-the-clock
durchnehmen*, to go
through, do, cover
dürfen, to be allowed to
(sich) **duschen**, to shower,
have/take a shower

ebenso ... wie, as ... as
die **Ecke**, corner
egal: das ist mir egal, I don't
mind, it's all the same to me
das **Ehepaar**, married couple
das **Ei** (-er), egg
eifrig, keen
eigen, own; **auf eigene
Gefahr**, at one's own risk
eigentlich, actually
sich **eignen für**, to be suitable for
eilen†, to hurry, hasten
eilig, quick(ly), swift(ly); **ich
habe es eilig**, I'm in a hurry
einatmen, to breathe in,
inhale
die **Einbahnstraße**, one-way
street
einfach, simple (-ly)

159

die **Einfahrt**, entrance, gateway, way in

einfallen*†, to occur to

sich **einfinden***, to be present, turn up

einholen, to catch up (with); get, obtain

einkaufen, to buy, purchase, shop

einladen*, to invite; load up

die **Einladung**, invitation

einlaufen*†, to arrive

sich **einleben**, to settle in

einmal, once, one day

einordnen, to get in lane

die **Einrichtung**, installations, fittings; equipment; furniture

einschecken, to check in

einschlafen*†, to fall asleep

einschränken, to confine, limit, restrict

die **Einschränkung**, restriction

einsteigen*†, to climb, get in

einstimmen, to agree, consent to

eintreffen*†, to arrive

eintreten*†, to step, walk in

die **Eintrittskarte** (-n), admission ticket

einverstanden, agreed

das **Einverständnis**, agreement, permission

einwerfen*, to post

Einzel-, single

die **Einzelheit** (-en), detail

einzeln, single (-ly), individual(ly)

die **Eisenbahn**, railway

die **Eisenstange**, iron bar

das **Eislaufen**, skating

das **Eisstadion**, ice rink

die **Eltern** (pl), parents

der **Elternsprechtag**, open day, 'parents' evening'

der **Empfang**, reception

empfehlen*, to recommend

endlich, finally, eventually, at last

das **Enkelkind** (-er), grandchild

entdecken, to discover

entfernen, to remove

entnehmen*, to take from, out of; withdraw

die **Entschuldigung**, apology; **Entschuldigung!** excuse me! sorry!

das **Entsetzen**, horror, dismay

entspannen, to relax

entweder ... oder, either ... or

entwerten, to cancel (ticket)

entziffern, to decipher

die **Erbse** (-n), pea

die **Erde**, earth, ground

das **Erdgeschoß**, ground floor

die **Erdkunde**, geography

sich **ereignen**, to happen

erfahren*, to experience; learn

die **Erfahrung** (-en), experience

der **Erfolg**, success

erfrischt, refreshed

die **Erfrischungen** (pl), refreshments

das **Ergebnis** (-se), result, outcome

erhalten*, to receive

erhältlich, available, obtainable

erheblich, considerable (-ly)

sich **erholen**, to recover, get better

sich **erinnern**, to remember

sich **erkälten**, to catch a cold

erkennen*, to recognize

erklären, to explain

sich **erkundigen (nach)**, to make enquiries about

erlauben, to allow, permit

die **Erlaubnis**, permission

erledigen, to deal with, finish off

erleichtert, relieved

erleiden*, to suffer, sustain, incur

erlügen*, to make up, invent, fabricate

ermüdet, tired (out)
ernst, serious(ly)
der Ernst, seriousness; ist das
dein Ernst? are you
serious?
die Erregung, excitement,
agitation, anger
erreichen, to reach
das Ersatzteil (-e), (spare) part
erscheinen*†, to appear
erschießen*, to shoot (dead)
erschöpft, exhausted
erschrocken, frightened,
scared, startled
erschüttern, to shake, upset
erst, first; only, not until
der Erwachsene §, grown-up,
adult
erwähnen, to mention
erwarten, to expect
erwidern, to reply
erzählen, to tell, relate
essen*, to eat
der Essig, vinegar
der Eßlöffel (-), dessert spoon
die Etage (-n), floor, storey
etwa, roughly, approximately,
about; perhaps, by any
chance
etwas, something; somewhat,
a bit
eventuell, possible (-ly);
perhaps
der Extrawagen, special coach

die Fabrik, factory
das Fach (-̈er), (school) subject;
compartment, locker,
pigeon-hole
die Fachnummer, locker number
die Fach(ober)schule, technical
college
die Fahrbahn, road, carriageway
lane
die Fähre, ferry
fahren*†, to go, drive, travel

die Fahrkarte (-n), ticket
der Fahrpreis, fare
der Fahrschein (-e), ticket
der Fahrstuhl, lift
falls, if, in case
fangen*, to catch
fast, almost
faul, lazy; bad (fruit etc.)
die Faust (-̈e), fist; die Fäuste
ballen, to clench one's fists
fegen, to sweep
fehlen, to be
missing/lacking/needed
der Fehler, mistake
feinfühlig, sensitive, tactful
die Ferien (pl), holidays
der Feriengast (-̈e), holidaymaker
fernsehen*, to watch
television
fest, firm; steady, regular
feststellen, to find out,
determine
die Feuchtigkeit, moisture,
humidity
das Feuerzeug, lighter
die Fichte (-n), spruce, fir tree
finden*, to find
der Fleischer, butcher
die Fleischerei, butcher's (shop)
der Fleiß, hard work
fleißig, hardworking
der Fleck (-e or -en), stain, spot
fliegen*†, to fly
fließen, to flow, run
fliehen*†, to flee, escape
flink, nimble, deft, quick,
sharp
die Flucht, flight, escape
das Fluchtauto, getaway car
flüchten†, to flee, escape
flüchtig, fleeting(ly)
der Flüchtling (-e), refugee
der Flug (-̈e), flight
die Flugangst, fear of flying
der Flughafen, airport
die Flugkarte (-n), plane ticket
das Flugzeug (-e), airplane

der **Flur**, corridor; hall
der **Fluß** (¨sse), river
die **Flußniederung**, fluvial plain
die **Folge** (-n), consequence,
   result
   folgen†, to follow
(das) **Frankreich**, France
   frei, free, unoccupied; **frei
   halten**, to keep clear
das **Freibad**, (outdoor) swimming
   pool
   Freien: im Freien, in the
   open air
die **Freizeit**, free time
die **Freizeitsbeschäftigung** (-en),
   hobby, pastime
   fremd, strange; foreign; **ich
   bin hier fremd**, I'm a
   stranger here
das **Fremdenverkehrsamt**, tourist
   office
das **Fremdenzimmer**, guest room,
   bed and breakfast
die **Fremdsprache** (-n), foreign
   language
   fressen*, to eat
sich **freuen (über)**, to be happy,
   pleased (about); **sich freuen
   auf**, to look forward to; **freut
   mich sehr!** pleased to meet
   you!
   frieren*, to freeze
der **Friseur, die Friseuse**,
   hairdresser
   froh, happy
   früh, early; **früher**, earlier,
   previous, former
das **Frühstück**, breakfast
   frühstücken, to have/eat
   breakfast
sich **fühlen**, to feel
das **Fundbüro**, lost property office
die **Fundgrube**, treasure
   trove/mine
die **Fundstelle**, (the place) where
   something is/was found
die **Fünf**, five (school grade)

   furchtbar, dreadful(ly)
   füttern, to feed

der **Gang**, corridor
   ganz, whole, entire; quite;
   completely
   gar, at all
das **Gasthaus** (¨er), **der Gasthof**
   (¨e), inn
das **Gebäude** (-), building
   geben*, to give
das **Gebiet** (-e), area, region,
   territory
   Gebraucht-, second hand
der **Geburtstag**, birthday
der **Gedanke‡** (-n), thought
die **Geduld**, patience
   geduldig, patient
   geeignet, suitable
die **Gefahr**, danger
   gefährlich, dangerous
   gefallen*, to please; **es
   gefällt mir**, I like it
das **Gefühl** (-e), feeling
   gegen, against; round about;
   **etwas gegen
   Kopfschmerzen**, something
   for headaches
die **Gegend**, area,
   neighbourhood, district
   gegenseitig, mutual(ly),
   reciprocal(ly)
das **Gegenteil**, opposite
   gehen*†, to go, walk
   gehören, to belong
die **Geige**, violin
das **Geld**, money
die **Geldstrafe**, fine
die **Gelegenheit** (-en),
   opportunity
die **Gelegenheitsanzeigen**, small
   ad(vertisement)s
   gelingen*, to succeed
   gelten*, to be valid
   gemeinsam, mutual(ly),
   joint(ly), together

das **Gemüse**, vegetable
gemütlich, comfortable, cosy; friendly
genau, exact(ly)
genauso ... wie, (just) as ... as
genießen*, to enjoy
genug, enough
das **Gepäck**, luggage
die **Gepäckaufbewahrung**, left-luggage office
gepflegt, well-groomed
gerade, just
geradeaus, straight ahead
geraten*†: **ins Schleudern geraten**, to get into a skid
das **Gericht** (-e), dish, meal; court(-house)
gering, low, slight, small
gern(e), with pleasure, willingly, readily; **ich schwimme gern**, I like swimming
die **Gesamtschule** (-n), comprehensive school
das **Geschäft** (-e), business, shop
geschäftlich, on business
geschehen*†, to happen
das **Geschenk** (-e), present
die **Geschichte**, story; history
das **Geschirr**, crockery
die **Geschwindigkeit**, speed
die **Geschwister** (pl), brothers and sisters
gesegnet, blessed; **gesegnete Mahlzeit!** for what we are about to receive may the Lord make us truly thankful
die **Gesellschaft**, society
das **Gesicht**, face
gespannt, taut; strained; eager(ly)
gesperrt, closed (of road, etc.)
das **Gespräch**, conversation
gestatten, to allow, permit

gestehen*, to confess, admit
gestern, yesterday
gesund, well, healthy
das **Getränk** (-e), drink
das **Gewächshaus**, greenhouse
das **Geweih** (-e), (set of) antlers
das **Gewicht**, weight
gewinnen*, to win
gewittern, to be stormy
gewittrig, stormy
gewöhnlich, usual(ly)
gewünscht, desired, required
gibt: es gibt, there is/are
gierig, greedy
der **Gipfel**, top, peak, summit
das **Gitterbett**, cot
der **Gitterzaun**, railing fence
der **Glanz**, gleam, shine, splendour, glare
das **Glatteis**, (black) ice
glauben, to believe
gleich, same, equal; immediately; just; **es ist mir gleich**, I don't mind, it's all the same to me
gleichfalls, likewise, also; at the same time
das **Gleis** (-e), line, platform
das **Glück**, luck, good fortune; **zum Glück**, fortunately
graben*, to dig
gratulieren, to congratulate
greifen*, to seize, grab, catch
die **Grenze** (-n), border
(das) **Griechenland**, Greece
die **Grippe**, influenza, 'flu
großartig, F. wonderful, splendid
die **Größe**, size, height
das **Großmaul**, big-mouth, loudmouth
der **Grund** (¨e), reason, grounds
grundsätzlich, in principle; absolutely
Grüne: ins Grüne, into the country(side)

der **Gruß** (⏜e), greeting
grüßen, to greet; **grüß Gott!**
hallo!
gucken, to look, peep
das **Gummi**, rubber
günstig, favourable,
convenient; reasonable
(price, etc.)
gurgeln, to gargle
gutbezahlt, well-payed
das **Gymnasium** (pl: **Gymnasien**),
grammar school

haben*, to have
das **Hackfleisch**, mince, minced
meat
der **Hafen**, harbour, port
das **Hallenbad**, indoor
swimming-pool
die **Halsschmerzen** (pl), sore
throat
halten*, to hold; stop; **halten
von**, to think of, reckon of
die **Haltestelle** (-n), stop
handeln, to act; trade,
bargain, haggle; **handeln
von, sich handeln um**, to be
about
die **Handfesseln** (pl), handcuffs
das **Handschuh** (-e), glove
das **Handschuhfach**, glove
compartment
das **Handtuch**, towel
hängen(*), to hang
(der) **Harz**, Harz mountains
häßlich, ugly; nasty, mean
häufig, often
Haupt-, chief, main, principal
die **Hauptstadt**, capital city
die **Hausaufgabe** (-n), homework
die **Haut**, skin
heben*, to lift
die **Hecke** (-n), hedge
heftig, violent(ly)
heil, unhurt, safe and sound
das **Heimweh**, homesickness

heiraten, to marry, get
married
heißen*, to be called, named
helfen*, to help
die **Herberge**, inn, hostel
Herren-, men's, gents'
herrlich, glorious, lovely,
magnificent
**Herrschaften: (meine)
Herrschaften!** ladies and
gentlemen
herstellen, to produce,
manufacture
hertreiben*: **vor sich
hertreiben**, to carry off,
away
das **Herz**, heart
herzlich, hearty (-ily),
cordial(ly)
herüberrufen, to call over
der **Heuschnupfen**, hay-fever
heute, today
hierher, here, to this place
die **Hilfe**, help
der **Hilferuf** (-e), cry for help
hilfsbereit, helpful, obliging
hinfallen*†, to fall over, down
sich **hinlegen**, to lie down
die **Hinreise**, the outward journey
der **Hintergrund**, background
hinterher, afterwards
der **Hinweis** (-e), advice, note, tip
der **Hirsch** (-e), deer
das **Hirschgeweih** (-e), (set of)
antlers
hitzefrei, off school (because
of excessively hot weather)
hocherfreut, highly delighted
das **Hochhaus** (⏜er),
high-rise/multi-storey
building
hocken, to sit around
der **Hof** (⏜e), (court)yard; farm
höflich, polite, courteous
hoffen, to hope
hoffentlich, hopefully, I (etc.)
hope

holen, to fetch
das **Holz**, wood
die **Holzhandlung**, timber firm
die **Hose** (-n), trousers
der **Hubschrauber** (-), helicopter
hupen, to hoot, sound one's horn

der **Imbiß**, snack
immer, always; **immer geradeaus**, keep straight on
die **Immobilien** (pl), property
indem, while, as; by (...ing)
infolge, as a result of, because of
der **Inhalt**, contents
die **Innenstadt**, town, city centre
innerhalb, inside, within
der **Insasse‡** (-n), occupant, passenger
die **Insel** (-n), island
insgesamt, altogether
das **Internat**, boarding school
irgend, some ... (or other)
sich **irren**, to make a mistake
der **Irrtum** (¨er), mistake

die **Jahreszeit** (-en), season
jeder, jede, jedes, each, every
der **Juckreiz**, itching
die **Jugend**, youth

der **Käfer** (-), beetle
kahl, bald; bare, bleak
der **Kamin**, fireplace
der **Kanal**, canal; (television) channel; English Channel
das **Kaninchen** (-), rabbit
kaputt, broken
die **Kartoffel** (-n), potato
der **Kassenzettel**, sales slip, receipt
der **Katzensprung**, F. stone's throw

der **Kellner, die Kellnerin**, waiter, waitress
kennen*, to know, be acquainted with
kennenlernen, to meet, make the acquaintance of
der **Kenner**, expert
das **Kfz. (Kraftfahrzeug)**, motor vehicle
das **Kino**, cinema
die **Kirchweih**, fair
die **Klamotten** (pl), F. clothes, gear, clobber
klappen, F. to work (out), be successful
das **Klavier**, piano
der **Kleiderschrank**, clothes cupboard, wardrobe
die **Kleidung**, clothes, clothing
das **Kleingeld**, (loose) change
klingen*, to sound
klug, intelligent, bright
der **Knall**, bang, sound (of a shot)
knapp, scarce, in short supply; barely sufficient; almost, very nearly
der **Kofferraum**, boot (of car)
der **Kohl**, cabbage
kommen*†, to come; **kommen lassen**, to send for
die **Konditorei**, confectioner's, cake shop
die **Königin**, queen
können*, to be able to
kontaktfreudig, (who) makes friends easily
kontrollieren, to check
der **Korb**, basket
der **Körper**, body
kostenpflichtig, at the owner's expense
das **Kraftwerk**, power station
die **Kräuter** (pl), herbs
die **Krawatte**, tie
kriegen, F. to get
die **Küche**, kitchen
der **Kühlschrank**, fridge, refrigerator

der **Kuli**, F. ball-point pen, 'biro'
sich **kümmern um**, to take care of
der **Kunde‡** (-n), **die Kundin**
   (-nen), customer, client
die **Kunst**, art
der **Kurs**, exchange rate
der **Kurswagen**, service bus
die **Küste**, coast
die **Kutsche**, coach

lächeln, to smile
lachen, to laugh
lächerlich, laughable, ridiculous
laden*, to load
der **Laden** (-̈), shop
das **Land** (-̈er), country; countryside
längst, for a long time now, a
   long time ago
sich **langweilen**, to be bored
langweilig, boring
der **Lärm**, noise, din, racket
lassen*, to leave; get/have
   (something done)
Lauf: im Laufe, in the course (of)
laufen*†, to run; go on foot
lauten, to read, go, be
läuten, to ring
lebenslustig, in love with life
die **Lebensmittel** (pl), food, groceries
das **Lebenszeichen** (-), sign of life
leer, empty
der **Lehrer** (-), **die Lehrerin**
   (-nen), teacher
die **Lehrkraft** (-̈e), teacher
der **Lehrling**, apprentice
leid: es tut mir leid, I'm sorry; **er
   tut mir leid**, I feel sorry for him
leiden*, to suffer; bear, tolerate
leider, unfortunately
leihen*, to lend; borrow
die **Leine**, line, rope; lead, leash
leise, quiet(ly), soft(ly), gentle (-ly)
sich **leisten: ich kann es mir
   nicht leisten**, I can't afford it
der **Leitpfahl**, post (along roadside)
das **Lenkrad**, steering wheel

lesen*, to read
der **Lesestoff**, reading material
die **Leute** (pl), people
lieber, rather, sooner
Liebes-, love
Lieblings-, favourite
liegen*, to lie, be lying;
   liegenlassen, to leave
der **Liegestuhl** (-̈e), deck-chair
lindern, to relieve, soothe
der **Linienbus**, service bus
der **Lkw (Lastkraftwagen)**, truck, lorry
locken, to entice, tempt, lure
locker, loose(ly), relaxed, in a
   relaxed fashion
der **Löffel** (-), spoon
los: was ist los? what's up,
   wrong; **es ist nicht viel los**,
   there's not much happening,
   going on
loslassen*, to let loose, unleash
die **Lösung**, remedy
die **Luftmatratze**, air-bed
Lust: Lust haben, to feel like,
   fancy
der **Lustspielfilm** (-e), comedy film

die **Mahlzeit** (-en), meal
die **Mahnung**, reminder
manchmal, sometimes
die **Mannschaft** (-en), team, crew
die **Marke** (-n), stamp
das **Meer**, sea(side)
das **Meerschweinchen** (-),
   guinea-pig
mehrere, several
die **Mehrfahrtenkarte** (-n),
   multi-journey ticket
mehrmals, several times
meiden*, to avoid
meinen, to think, reckon; say,
   remark
die **Meinung**, opinion; **meiner
   Meinung nach**, in my opinion
meistens, mostly, for the most
   part

sich **melden**, to report, check in, answer, announce one's presence

die **Menge**, crowd; quantity

der **Mensch‡** (-en), person, human being

merken, to notice, realize, remember

der **Metzger**, butcher

die **Metzgerei**, butcher's (shop)

mieten, to hire, rent

der **Mieter, die Mieterin**, tenant; lodger

mindestens, at least

mißlingen*, to fail, be unsuccessful

die **Mitarbeit**, co-operation

das **Mitglied** (-er), member

mitteilen, to inform

die **Möbel** (pl), furniture

das **Mofa** (-s), small moped

mögen*, to like; **es mag sein**, it might be

möglich, possible

die **Möglichkeit** (-en), possibility

momentan, at the moment

der **Monat** (-e), month

müde, tired

die **Mühe**, trouble, bother, effort; **die Mühe wert**, worth the trouble; **sich viel Mühe geben**, to take great pains

die **Münze** (-n), coin

der **Münztank**, coin-operated petrol pump

müssen*, must, to have to

der **Nachbar‡** (-n), **die Nachbarin** (-nen), neighbour

nachgehen*†, to go after, follow

nachlassen*, to decrease, ease off

der **Nachname‡**, surname

die **Nachricht** (-en), (piece of) news

nachschauen, to look at, check

der **Nachtisch**, dessert, pudding

der **Nachttopf**, (chamber) pot

die **Nadel** (-n), needle

Nadel-, conifer(ous)

nagelneu, brand new

die **Nähe**, neighbourhood, proximity

Näheres, further details

der **Nahverkehrszug**, local train

naß, wet

der **Nebel**, fog

neb(e)lig, foggy

das **Nebenzimmer**, adjoining room

nehmen*, to take

nennen*, to name

nett, nice

neulich, recently

nichts, nothing

niederländisch, Dutch

nie(mals), never

niesen, to sneeze

der **Niesreiz**, itchy nose

nippen, to sip

noch, still, even; more, else, other; some time, one day

Nord-, north, northern

Not-, emergency

notwendig, necessary

nur, only

ob, whether

oben, upstairs, at the top, up

oberst-, topmost, very top

die **Oberstufe**, upper school, sixth form

das **Obst**, fruit

obwohl, although

offensichtlich, obvious(ly)

öffnen, to open

ohne, without

das **Opfer** (-), sacrifice

die **Ordnung**, order; **in Ordnung**, all right, OK

der **Ort**, place, spot

Ost-, east, eastern

Oster-, Ostern, Easter

(das) **Österreich**, Austria

ein **paar**, a few
das **Paar** (-e), pair
die **Panne**, breakdown
passen, to fit, suit, go with; be
  suitable, convenient
passieren†, to happen
die **Pause**, break
Pech: Pech haben, to be
  unlucky
die **Pension** (-en), guest-house
der **Pfad**, path
die **Pfeife**, pipe
das **Pferdereiten**, horse-riding
Pfingst-, Pfingsten, Whit(sun)
pflücken, to pick
das **Pfund**, pound
der **Pilz** (-e), mushroom
die **Piste**, runway; track; (ski) run
planmäßig, scheduled
die **Platte** (-n), record
plaudern, to chat
die **Plombe**, filling (in tooth)
plötzlich, suddenly
der **Pokal**, cup, trophy
die **Polizeistreife**, police patrol
das **Portemonnaie**, purse
die **Postkutsche**, mail coach,
  stagecoach
postwendend, by return (of
  post)
das **Postwertzeichen** (-),
  (postage) stamp
prallen† (gegen), to crash (into)
das **Präsidium**, (police) headquarters
das **Preisausschreiben**, competition
preisgünstig, inexpensive
das **Preisrätsel**, prize competition
preiswert, good value
die **Probefahrt**, test drive
probieren, to try
prüfen, to test, examine
die **Prüfung** (-en), test, examination
pünktlich, punctual(ly)
die **Puppe**, doll
putzen, to clean, scrub, polish,
  wipe; **sich die Zähne putzen**,
  to clean/brush one's teeth

qm (Quadratmeter), square
  metre
der **Quatsch**, rubbish
die **Quittung**, receipt

radeln†, to cycle
das **Rad** (¨er), wheel; bicycle
der **Rand**, edge, side, rim
die **Rangelei**, scuffle, fight
rasch, quick(ly)
der **Rasen**, lawn
der **Rat**, advice
raten*, to advise; guess
das **Rathaus**, town hall
rauchen, to smoke
reagieren, to react
rechnen mit, to reckon on
die **Rechnung**, bill
recht: recht haben, to be right
rechtzeitig, (just) in time, in
  good time, on time
reden, to speak, talk
regelmäßig, regular(ly)
der **Regen**, rain
reichlich, ample (-ly), richly
der **Reifen** (-), tyre
die **Reifenpanne**, burst tyre, puncture
das **Reiheneckhaus**, end
  terrace-house
rein, clean
die **Reinigung**, cleaning
das **Reisebüro**, travel agency
der **Reisende** §, traveller
die **Reisepost**, (post) bus service
reißen*, to tear, rip; seize, snatch
reiten*†, to ride
reklamieren, to complain,
  make a complaint
Renn-, racing
rennen*†, to run
der **Rentner** (-), old-age
  pensioner, senior citizen
retten, to save
der **Rettungshubschrauber**,
  rescue helicopter
das **Rezept**, recipe; prescription

rezeptfrei, over-the-counter, not requiring a prescription

rezeptpflichtig, only available on prescription

die **Richtung** (-en), direction

riesengroß, huge, gigantic, enormous

die **Rinde**, bark

ringsum, (all) around

der **Rock** (¨e), skirt

die **Rolltreppe**, escalator, moving staircase

die **Rübe** (-n), turnip

der **Rücken**, back

die **Rückkehr**, return

das **Rückspiel**, return match

rufen*, to call

die **Ruhe**, peace, quiet; calm(ness)

die **Rundfahrt**, tour, round trip

rutschen†, to slip

die **Sachen** (pl), things, belongings

sammeln, to collect

der **Sammelumkleideraum**, mixed changing-room

satt: es satt haben, to be fed up with

saugen*, to suck

die **Säure**, acid

schade, shame; **wie schade!** what a shame!

schaden, to harm, damage

schaffen: es schaffen, to make, manage it

der **Schaffner**, ticket-collector, guard

die **Schallplatte** (-n), record

schätzen, to estimate, guess, reckon

schauen, to look

die **Schaukel**, swing

die **Scheibe**, (window-)pane; slice; turntable

scheiden*, to separate, divorce

der **Schein** (-e), note, bill; ticket

scheinen*, to shine; seem

schenken, to give (as a present)

scheußlich, dreadful, hideous

die **Schichtarbeit**, shift work

schick, elegant, chic

schicken, to send

schiefgehen*†, to go wrong

das **Schild**, signpost, name-plate, number-plate

schlafen*, to sleep

der **Schlafsack** (¨e), sleeping bag

schlagen*, to hit, beat

der **Schlager** (-), hit (record)

die **Schlange**, snake; queue

schleppen, to tow, pull, drag

der **Schleuder**, spin-drier

schleudern†, to skid

schließen*, to close, shut

schließlich, finally, lastly

schlimm, bad

das **Schloß** (pl: **Schlösser**), castle, palace, stately home

der **Schlot** (-e), chimney

Schluß: Schluß machen, to finish, call it a day

der **Schlüssel** (-), key

schmecken, to taste (good)

schmerzen, to hurt

schminken, to make up

der **Schmuck**, jewellery

schmutzig, dirty

der **Schnee**, snow

schneiden*, to cut

der **Schnellimbiß**, snack bar

die **Schnulze** (-n), F. slushy, sentimental film, etc.

die **Schnur**, string, thread

schon, already

der **Schrank** (¨e), cupboard

die **Schranke**, barrier, gate

schreiben*, to write

schreien*, to scream, shout

der **Schriftführer**, secretary (of club, etc.)

schriftlich, in writing, written

schrottreif, only fit for scrap, 'written off'

die **Schublade** (-n), drawer
schulden, to owe
der **Schuppen**, shed
der **Schuß**, (pl. Schüsse), shot
die **Schüssel** (-n), bowl
schütteln, to shake
der **Schutz**, shelter, cover
schwach, weak
schwärmen (für), to be wild, crazy (about)
schwerbehindert, severely handicapped
der **Schwiegersohn**, son-in-law
die **Schweiz**, Switzerland
die **Schwierigkeit** (-en), difficulty, problem
das **Schwimmbecken**, swimming pool
sechzig, sixty; **in den sechziger Jahren**, in the sixties
seekrank, seasick
sehen*, to see, look
sei! seid! seien Sie! be!
das **Seil**, rope
sein*, to be
die **Selbstschußanlage**, booby-trap device
selbstständig, independent
selbstverständlich, of course, obvious(ly)
seltsam, strange, odd
senden(*), to send, broadcast
der **Sendeschluß**, end of transmission
die **Sendung** (-en), (television) programme
seufzen, to sigh
sicher, sure, certain
die **Sicherheit**, security, safety
der **Sicherheitsgurt** (-e), seat-belt, safety-belt
die **Sichtweite**, visibility
sitzen*, to sit, be sitting
so ... wie, as ... as
sowieso, anyway, in any case
sofort, at once, immediately

sollen*, to be supposed to; ought
das **Sonderangebot** (-e), special offer
der **Sonnenaufgang**, sunrise
der **Sonnenbrand**, sunburn
sonst, otherwise, (or) else; **sonst noch etwas?** is/was there anything else?
die **Sorge** (-n), worry; **sich Sorgen machen um**, to be concerned about
sorgfältig, careful(ly)
die **Sorten** (pl), foreign currency; **Sorten-Kurse**, foreign currency exchange rates
sowohl ... als (auch) ..., both ... and ...
spannend, exciting, thrilling
sparen, to save
die **Sparkasse**, savings bank
der **Spaß**, fun
spazierenfahren*†, to go for a drive
spazierengehen*†, to go for a walk
die **Speise**, food
die **Speisekarte**, menu
der **Speisewagen**, restaurant car
sperren, to close (off)
das **Sperrgebiet**, prohibited area
der **Spiegel**, mirror
das **Spielgerät**, apparatus (for playing on)
die **Spielwaren** (pl), toys
die **Spitze**, tip, top, peak; **Spitze!** F. great! fantastic!
die **Spitzenlage**, prime site
spottbillig, dirt cheap
sprechen*, to speak
die **Sprechstunden, Sprechzeiten** (pl), consulting times
springen*†, to jump
sprühen, to spray
spülen, to rinse, wash (up)
die **Spur** (-en), track, trace; lane
das **Stadion** (pl: **Stadien**), stadium

der **Stadtbummel**, stroll in/through town

stammen aus, to come from

ständig, constant(ly)

stark, strong(ly), heavy (-ily)

statt, instead of

stattfinden*, to take place

der **Stau** (-e or -s), (traffic) jam, tailback

stehen*, to stand, be standing; **es steht dir gut**, it fits you; **es steht gut um ihn**, things look good for him

stehlen*, to steal

steigen*†, to climb, mount

steil, steep

stellen, to put, stand; catch

das **Stellengesuch** (-e), 'employment wanted' advertisement

die **Stellung**, position, post, situation

stempelngehen, to be, go on the dole

sterben*†, to die

das **Steuer**, steering-wheel

Stich: im Stich lassen*, to leave in the lurch

der **Stiefel** (-), boot

die **Stimme**, voice

stimmen, to be right, correct

die **Stimmung**, mood

stinklangweilig, F. deadly boring, dull

der **Stock** (¨e), stick

der **Stock, das Stockwerk** (pl: **Stockwerke**), storey, floor

stolpern†, to stumble, trip

stolz (auf), proud (of)

stören, to disturb, bother

die **Störung**, disturbance, disruption

störungsfrei, moving freely (again)

stoßen*, to push, shove

der **Strafzettel**, (traffic) ticket

der **Strand**, beach

strapaziert, worn out, exhausted

die **Strecke**, distance; road; way, route

streichen*, to stroke; spread

das **Streichholz** (¨er), match

der **Streifenwagen** (-), patrol car

streng, strict(ly), severe(ly)

Strömen: in Strömen regnen, to be pouring (with rain)

stürzen†, to rush, dash; fall, plunge

Süd-, south, southern

die **Süßwaren** (pl), sweets

sympathisch, pleasant, nice

die **Tagesschau**, (television) news

täglich, daily

die **Tankstelle** (-n), petrol station

der **Tankwart**, petrol pump attendant

die **Tasche** (-n), pocket, bag

die **Taschendieb** (-e), pickpocket

das **Taschengeld,**, pocket money

die **Taste** (-n), button

der **Täter**, culprit, person responsible

die **Tatort**, scene of the crime

tatsächlich, in fact, actually

die **Taube** (-n), dove

tauschen, to exchange, swap

teilen, to share

teilnehmen* (an), to take part (in)

teilweise, in part, partly

der **Termin**, date, appointment

teuer, dear, expensive

tief, deep

die **Tiefgarage**, (underground) car park

das **Tier** (-e), animal

der **Tierarzt** (¨e), **die Tierärztin** (-nen), vet(erinary surgeon)

der **Tod**, death; **zu Tode**, to death

tödlich, fatal, deadly, lethal

toll, mad; **toll!** F. great!

die **Tollwut**, rabies

der **Topf** (¨e), pot

tot, dead

totschlagen*, to kill

tragen*, to carry; wear

trampen†, F. to hitch(-hike)
der **Traum** (¨e), dream
traurig, sad
sich **treffen* (mit)**, to meet (up with one another);
Vorbereitungen treffen, to make preparations
der **Treffpunkt**, meeting-place, rendezvous
treiben*, to drive; **Sport treiben**, to do/go in for sport
treten*†, to step, kick
treu, faithful(ly)
der **Trimm-Dich-Pfad**, keep-fit course/trail
trinken*, drink
trocken, dry
trocknen, to dry
die **Tropfsteinhöhle**, cave (with stalagmites and stalactites)
trotz, in spite of
trotzdem, still, nevertheless, in spite of that
tschüs(chen)! F. cheerio! 'bye! so long!
tun*, to do
die **Tür** (-en), door
turnen, to do gymnastics
das **Turnhemd**, gym/PE shirt
die **Tüte**, (plastic/paper) bag
der **TÜV (Technischer Überwachungs-Verein)**, MOT

die **U-Bahn**, underground, tube
üben, to practise, exercise
die **Überfahrt**, crossing
der **Überfall**, raid
überhaupt, at all
überhöht, excessive
überlassen*, to leave it (up) to, entrust
überlegen, to think (over)
übernachten, to spend the night, stay
die **Übernachtung**, overnight stay
überqueren, to cross

überrascht, surprised
sich **überschlagen***, to somersault, turn over
die **Überschwemmung** (-en), flood
übersenden*: hiermit übersenden wir Ihnen ..., please find enclosed ...
überwinden*, to overcome, get over
üblich, usual(ly)
übrig, (left) over, remaining
die **Übung**, practice, exercise
das **Ufer** (-), bank, shore
die **Uhr**, clock, watch; o'clock
sich **umdrehen**, to turn round
umfahren*, to run/knock over/down
die **Umgebung**, surroundings, area
der **Umkleideraum**, changing room
die **Umleitung**, diversion
umstoßen*, to knock over
der **Umtausch**, exchange
umwechseln, to change
sich **umziehen***, to get changed
der **Umzug**, move, removal
undenkbar, unthinkable
der **Unfall** (¨e), accident
(das) **Ungarn**, Hungary
ungefähr, approximately, about
ungestört, undisturbed
die **Unruhe**, noise, disturbance
die **Unschuld**, innocence
unterbringen*, to accommodate, put up
sich **unterhalten* (mit)**, to converse with
die **Unterhaltung**, talk, chat, conversation; entertainment
die **Unterkunft**, accommodation, lodging
unternehmen*, to undertake, do
der **Unterricht**, instruction, teaching
die **Unterrichtsstunde** (-n), lesson, class

untersagt, forbidden, prohibited

unterstützen, to support

untersuchen, to investigate, examine

die **Untertitel** (pl), subtitles

unterwegs, on the way, underway, on the road

unwohl, unwell, uneasy

der **Urlaub**, holiday

ursprünglich, original(ly)

sich **verabschieden**, to take one's leave

sich **verändern**, to change

verärgert, angry

verbinden*, to tie, bandage up; unite, join together

der **Verbot**, ban

verboten, forbidden

verbrauchen, to use up

verbringen*, to spend (time)

verdammt, F. damned

verdienen, to earn; deserve

der **Verein**, club

vereinigt, united; **die Vereinigten Staaten**, United States

verfehlen, to miss

verfolgen, to pursue, hunt

Verfügung: zur Verfügung stehen, to be at someone's disposal; **zur Verfügung stellen**, to put at someone's disposal

vergebens, in vain

vergehen*†, to pass

vergessen*, to forget

das **Vergnügen**, pleasure

verheiraten, to marry

verhungern†, to die of hunger

der **Verkehr**, traffic

verkehren (mit), to mix with

die **Verkehrslage**, traffic situation

die **Verkehrsstockung** (-en), traffic hold-up

der **Verkehrsverein**, tourist information office

verlassen*, to leave

verlegen, embarrassed

verlegen, to mislay

(sich) **verletzen**, to injure, hurt (oneself)

verlieren*, to lose

sich **verloben**, to get engaged

die **Vermietung**, renting (out), hiring (out)

vermuten, to suspect, assume, presume

vermutlich, presumably

verpassen, to miss

verreisen†, to go away (on a trip)

verschenken, to give away

verscheuchen, to scare off, away

verschieden, different

sich **verschlafen***, to oversleep

verschließen*, to lock (up)

verschwinden*†, to disappear

die **Versicherung**, insurance

die **Verspätung**, delay

verständigen, to notify, advise

das **Verständnis**, understanding, sympathy

verstecken, to hide

verstehen*, to understand

versuchen, to attempt, try

vertragen*, to tolerate, stand, endure

vertrauen, to trust, have trust in

verunglücken†, to have an accident

verunsichern, to make unsure, uncertain

der **Verwandte** §, relation, relative

verwöhnen, to spoil

verwundert, amazed, astonished

verzeihen*, to forgive

verzollen, to declare

viel(e), much, a lot, many

vielleicht, perhaps

die **Viertelstunde** (-n), a quarter of an hour

das **Visum** (pl: **Visa** or **Visen**), visa

völlig, completely
vollkommen, perfect(ly)
vor, in front of; before; ago
voraussichtlich, expected, probable (-ly)
der **Vorbeigehende** §, passer-by
vorbeischauen, F. to call in, drop by
vorbereiten, to prepare
die **Vorbereitung** (-en), preparation
Vorder-, front, fore
vorhaben*, to intend, have planned
vorher, previously
vorig, last, previous
vorkommen*†, to appear, seem
vorliegen*: **es muß ein Irrtum vorliegen**, there must be a mistake
vormittags, in the morning
vorn(e), at the front
der **Vorname**‡ (-n), first, Christian name
vornehm, smart, posh
der **Vorort** (-e), suburb
der **Vorschlag** (¨e), suggestion
vorschlagen*, to suggest
die **Vorsicht**, care, attention
vorsichtig, careful(ly)
die **Vorspeise** (-n), hors-d'oeuvre, 'starter'
die **Vorstadt**, suburbs
der **Vorsteher**, station-master
(sich) **vorstellen**, to introduce (oneself)
die **Vorstellung** (-en), performance
der **Vorverkauf**, advance booking
vorzeigen, to show, produce

wachsen*†, to grow
während, during; while, whereas
wahr, true
wahrnehmen*: **die Gelegenheit wahrnehmen**, to take, avail oneself of the opportunity
wahrscheinlich, probable (-ly)
der **Wald** (¨er), wood
wandern†, to hike, walk

die **Wanderung**, hike, walk
die **Wanne**, bath(-tub)
der **Warenumtausch**, exchange of goods
(sich) **waschen***, to wash (oneself)
waten†, to wade
wechseln, to change, exchange
die **Wechselstube** (-n), exchange office
weder ... noch ..., neither ... nor ...
wegen, because, on account of
weh: weh tun, to hurt
sich **wehren**, to defend oneself
Weihnachten, Weihnachts-, Christmas
weinen, to cry
die **Weise**, way
weisen*, to show
weit, far
sich **wenden*** **(an)**, to turn (to)
wenig(e), little, few; **immer weniger**, less and less
werden*†, to become, get
werfen*, to throw
der **Werkunterricht**, woodwork and metalwork, etc., CDT
die **Wertsachen** (pl), valuables
wessen? whose?
der **Wettkampf**, competition
wichtig, important
wiederholen, to repeat
wiederstehen*, to resist
wiegen*, to weigh
das **Wildleder**, suede (leather)
winseln, to whimper
wirklich, really
wissen*, to know
der **Witz** (-e), joke
die **Woche** (-n), week
woher? where from? how?
wohin? where (to)?
wohl, well; presumably; **zum Wohl!** cheers!
die **Wohlfahrtsmarke** (-n), charity stamp
der **Wohnort**, place of residence

die **Wohnsiedlung**, estate
die **Wohnung** (-en), flat
der **Wohnwagen** (-), caravan
womöglich, possibly
wozu? for what purpose? why?
würzig, tasty, spicy
wütend, furious

zähflüssig, slow-moving
die **Zahlung** (-en), payment
der **Zahn** (¨e), tooth
der **Zahnarzt** (¨e), **die Zahnärztin**
(-nen), dentist
die **Zapfsäule** (-n), petrol pump
der **Zebrastreifen**, zebra crossing
zeigen, to show
die **Zeile** (-n), line
die **Zeit**, time; **zu der Zeit**, at that
time, then
die **Zeitschrift** (-en), magazine
die **Zeitung** (-en), newspaper
das **Zeitungsinserat** (-e),
newspaper advertisement
das **Zelt** (-e), tent
zelten, to camp
zerfressen*, to eat away
zerschneiden*, to cut (up)
der **Zettel**, piece of paper, card,
chit, ticket
der **Zeuge‡** (-n), **die Zeugin**
(-nen), witness

das **Zeugnis**, (school) report
ziehen*, to pull, draw
die **Ziehung**, draw
das **Ziel**, goal, aim, destination
ziemlich, quite
zittern, to tremble
der **Zoll**, customs
der **Zöllner** (-), customs officer
zu, to, at; closed
das **Zubehör**, accessories
zufrieden, satisfied
der **Zug** (¨e), train
die **Zukunft**, future
zunächst, first(ly)
die **Zündung**, ignition
zurückbekommen*, to get back
zusammenlegen, to club
together, have a 'whip round'
zusammenstellen, to arrange
zusammensuchen, to collect
(together)
der **Zuschauer** (-), spectator,
viewer, member of audience
der **Zuschlag**, surcharge, supplement
zuschlagpflichtig, subject to
a supplement
zuschließen*, to lock (up)
der **Zustand**, state, condition
zuteilen, to allocate
der **Zweck** (-e), purpose
zwischendurch, in the mean
time

Grammar index